Preparing for the Bar Exam

A Comprehensive Guide to Plans, Programs, Content, Conditions, and Skills

Nelson P. Miller and Douglas A. Johnson

Preparing for the bar exam: a comprehensive guide to plans, programs, content, conditions, and skills.

Miller, Nelson P., and Douglas A. Johnson

Published by:

Crown Management LLC – August 2015

1527 Pineridge Drive
Grand Haven, MI 49417
USA

ISBN: 978-0-9905553-8-4

For examinees who want to pass the bar — on the first try.

Table of Contents

Detailed Table of Contents

Introduction

Requirement

While rare locales recognize exceptions, ordinarily you *must* pass a bar exam to obtain a state bar's license to practice law as a lawyer in that jurisdiction. You may earn Juris Doctor or Master of Laws degrees without passing a bar exam, but you must pass the bar to practice law as a licensed lawyer. Passing the bar exam is not the only action that state bars will require of you for licensure. You will also need to register for and apply to the bar while also demonstrating your character and fitness to practice law. Depending on the particular state's requirements, you may need to pass the Multistate Professional Responsibility Exam within a certain period before or after passing the bar exam. Choosing or at least projecting your state of practice is thus a critical first step in preparing for the bar exam. Until you choose the state in which you plan to obtain a law license, you cannot be sure of what licensing exams you must take and what subjects will be on those exams. Once you choose a state, with an online search of the state-bar website you can learn your state bar's licensure requirements early so that you can plan accordingly. Taking early action can save you time and money later. In some states, you can save considerable fees by registering for your state bar when beginning law school or shortly after. No matter what state in which you choose to license, you may save time, trouble, and treasure by taking law school courses in bar-tested subjects. You may also save time and trouble by taking the Multistate Professional Responsibility Exam while still in law school shortly after studying lawyer conduct rules.

Plan

If you have not already done so, then consider creating a master schedule now for your licensure, including preparing for and passing the bar exam, even if you are just starting law school. Graduating from law school with a Juris Doctor degree is a tremendous accomplishment, one that you should fully enjoy. Enjoying graduation is difficult, though, when the bar exam looms not too long after graduation and you have not adequately planned for your bar-exam preparation. Thorough planning and early preparation can turn the prospect of the bar exam from a dark specter clouding your graduation celebration to a welcome once-in-a-lifetime challenge for which you know you will be prepared and believe you are entirely worthy. Counteract fear and anxiety with a plan. Planning makes the difference in the success of your bar-exam preparation. Examinees don't pass because their plans leave gaps in their skills and knowledge. Moreover, unlike preparing for any of your law school exams, *you personally*, rather than someone else, need to plan for your bar-exam preparation. You have no professor to plan for you, you have no assigned casebook telling you what to study, and yet you must be able to give specific rapid-fire answers to dozens of law problems. After checking your state bar's requirements online, include in your master schedule the dates that you plan to complete each of the following activities that your state bar may encourage or require:

- update law school application;
- register with the state bar;
- apply to the state bar;
- submit character-and-fitness materials;
- complete mini or baby bar exam;
- pass Multistate Professional Responsibility Exam;
- register for commercial bar-preparation course;
- graduate from law school;
- engage fully and effectively in bar-exam preparation; and
- complete the bar exam confidently and competently.

Complexity

Now set those preliminaries aside to consider the task of actually preparing for the bar exam. Passing the bar requires a much more varied and complex set of attitudes, practices, disciplines, activities, and efforts than most examinees initially appreciate. You may think that bar passage simply requires you to invest a considerable amount of time. While there is some truth to this assumption, successful preparation requires much more than simply investing time. Effective bar preparation involves many more activities than simply staring for hours at videos, summaries, and outlines. You cannot hope to achieve bar passage by being passive in your efforts. Bar passage takes concerted, focused, effective, and varied effort of a kind you have probably never attempted, to regain, integrate, and improve upon the knowledge and skills that you learned in law school, to do well on a specialized licensing exam. Because of the extraordinary size, focus, and comprehensiveness of the effort required, your bar-exam preparation will require you to develop, expand, and fully exercise a variety of learning and self-management skills that you may have only so far begun to explore. An underappreciated value of the bar-exam experience is that you are learning to identify, develop, organize, implement, and assess a wide range of disciplines, resources, attitudes, and activities around a single hugely worthwhile goal. Doing bar preparation right should forever change you for the better because of that integrative varied effort.

Organization

Look, for instance, at the chapter headings in this book. If you don't realize it already, then you will soon discover that your *mindset* is hugely important to your success. The bar-exam challenge is large enough that if you don't have your attitude right, then you may make the experience much more difficult and less rewarding than you should. Similarly, if you are not thoughtful and intentional about your *health* while preparing for the bar exam, then you will suffer more physical, mental, and emotional stress than you should. Likewise, if you don't attend to and manage your *relationships* in the way that you can and should, then you will not have the social support that you need to thrive under challenging circumstance. Your *schedule* and willingness and ability to keep to it is more important than ever during bar preparation. The list goes on. Knowing the exam's *content* is hugely important to your success, but so is knowing the exam's *format*, the *conditions* under which you will take the exam, and the way in which you *manage* those conditions. Your *practice* of the skills that the bar exam requires is key to your success. Your skill at *multiple-choice* and *essay* questions is of course critical. Your *behavior* throughout the bar-preparation process has surprising influences on your success. How you manage bar-exam *results* can also be more important than you think. This book addresses each of those subjects.

Process

Appreciate that passing the bar exam involves following a multi-faceted process. Know the process to get the results. To pass the bar, draw on and hone the skills that you learned for law practice. You wouldn't try a jury case without knowing and preparing for the order of trial, just as you wouldn't conduct a closing or handle a business acquisition or merger without knowing the closing, acquisition, or merger process. When you treat preparing for the bar as thoughtfully and responsibly as you would treat any other professional activity, you confirm your best professional practices while maximizing your success. Don't pass the bar barely after an anxious, harrowing, or even debilitating process that leaves you without confidence and with a bad taste for law practice. Instead, pass the bar easily because you made a full-time commitment to do so and then gave your effort appropriate structure and thought. An Association of American Law Schools study from some years ago urged law schools to help students prepare earlier for the bar exam not just in acquiring necessary doctrinal knowledge but in developing the life skills that examinees must reflect to prepare adequately. Bar preparation empowers you to accomplish other valuable things in your career and life long after you have passed the bar exam. Indeed, in bar-exam preparation, you should be learning a new way to challenge and encourage yourself to accomplish greater things in the future than passing a very challenging licensing exam.

Challenge

In preparing for the bar exam, you have indeed accepted a wonderful challenge, one of the great intellectual and professional challenges available today. Courage is not the absence of fear but the willing to face and overcome it. Face and resolve your fear of

4

the bar exam now, rather than later. Consider why examinees fear the bar exam and how you can both relieve that fear and replace it with deliberate preparation toward passing. The bar exam's first challenge is its breadth. You may have the impression that the bar exam tests so many subjects and so much law that you cannot possibly learn enough law to control confidently your prospects for passing. Actually, though, the bar exam tests only certain law fields, omitting many other fields to which law school may have exposed you or that you may encounter in practice. Bar examiners also list for you tested topics and subtopics within those fields. With appropriate investigation, you will know the law fields and topics, and can prepare accordingly for a manageable challenge. A second concern that examinees reflect is that they don't have time to prepare. Actually, though, few examinees genuinely lack the time, especially considering that you can spread your bar-exam preparation out over a long enough period to manage your other responsibilities even as you prepare for the bar. Examinees who run out of time or feel inordinate time pressure tend to be those who did not plan and manage their time adequately. With proper action, you can manage not only the bar's subjects but your preparation time.

Small Steps

The last concern that examinees tend to express has to do with the bar exam's high stakes including the consequences of not passing. The bar exam may seem like such a lofty goal as to be intimidating and beyond your capabilities. If you feel yourself becoming overwhelmed by the big picture, then it may help you to conceptualize bar preparation as a series of many little steps rather than a single huge obstacle. Every great sculpture was made one chisel stroke at a time. No one was born a great lawyer; even the most admirable legal scholars in history learned their craft in small individual pieces. At any given moment you have only one small and manageable step immediately in front of you. By earning a law degree, you proved that you have the capability to pass the bar. You have already proven that you largely control your outcome in passing the bar exam. Prepare earnestly, wisely, and effectively, and your outcome will be the great reward of passing. That great reward is why the bar exam has such high stakes. Let those high stakes spur you on to preparing. And then just take your preparation one sure step at a time.

1 Strategy

Strategy Matters

Bar preparation is very likely to be the most strategic individual activity that you ever do. Sure, if you become a trial lawyer conducting high-stakes litigation, or a deal lawyer handling complex transactions, then you will spend your career involved in highly strategic work. Yet no matter how high the stakes and how complex the transaction, practice remains vocation, *work* that you do *in conjunction with others* and *focused on known specific matters*. By contrast, the bar exam is entirely and solely about *you*, not about client matters and not something that you do coordinating with others. You alone matter, and you alone do the work. The bar exam is also not about a specific known matter but about *every possible unknown* legal matter within multiple vast fields. Given the peculiar nature of the bar exam's challenge that you alone must prepare for a great unknown, your preparation must be strategic to be effective. You cannot simply flail away at whatever occurs to you on any given day in your preparation. You must be programmatic, thoughtful, and deliberate in your planning and preparation.

Developing Tactics

The specific study tactics that you employ, like reviewing one subject and writing one related practice essay in the morning and another subject and essay in the afternoon each day before concluding with multiple-choice questions, or similar plans, matter most. Because the stages of your preparation will change as you move from law review to more and more practice, you will start with one specific study tactic but adopt other tactics over time. Your ability and willingness to modify tactics as you proceed, in itself a key strategy, will largely determine your study effectiveness. One tactic will be highly effective for a period before becoming ineffective, while another tactic will replace it as most effective at your preparation stage. You will read or hear of many different bar-preparation tactics whether in law school programs or from commercial bar-preparation programs or fellow examinees. None are magic bullets. Any of them may have merit at one point in your studies, while others may have merit at other points. The point is that you must adopt and adapt these tactics throughout your studies. Consider the following two examples of specific study tactics before reading about some broader strategies that can contribute to your success:

- begin each day with a timed bank of multiple-choice questions, reviewing answer explanations immediately after you finish, then move to lower-energy video and reading review, then move back to higher-engagement timed essay practice on the reviewed subject, reviewing model answers as soon as you finish, then in the afternoon repeat the same cycle but on a different subject, until you have covered all subjects, then repeat;
- begin each day with video review, reading, outlining, flash cards, and other study of a Multistate Bar Examination subject, then do a bank of related multiple-choice questions, then write a related essay answer, then in the afternoon repeat the cycle for a state-specific subject not on the Multistate Bar Examination, before spending the end of the day reviewing and critiquing your performance on both subjects.

Goals and Objectives

Adopt and pursue goals. Setting goals can be critical to successful performance. The obvious goal that anyone taking the bar exam should adopt is to *pass the bar exam*. Make passing the bar exam your goal. You might be surprised how many examinees do not actually adopt bar passage as their goal. Listen carefully to others who are planning to take the bar exam, and you will hear some of them saying that they just plan to give the bar exam a try to see how well they can do on it without adequately preparing. Do not be one of those examinees. Make your goal to *pass*, not just to *take*, the bar exam. Candidly, *taking* the bar exam is actually in itself a substantial challenge and in that respect a laudable goal. But taking the bar exam is laudable only when you combine doing so with the goal to *pass*. To take the bar exam without the goal to pass the bar exam is more like masochism than reason. Yet you could adopt the goal not just to pass the bar exam but to *ace* the bar exam, or to clobber, dominate, or overwhelm it. Set high-enough goals for yourself that you reduce the risk of not passing the bar exam. Set goals that challenge and inspire you, not ones that imply merely surviving it. If your only goal is to pass, then you may or may not do so, just barely. If your goal is to *shine* on the bar exam, then you may have just substantially increased your likelihood of passing. Then, set not only your overarching goal but intermediate objectives. You may, for instance, benefit from monthly, weekly, and daily objectives. When you set an objective for the day's preparation such as to complete review of a certain subject and then practice a certain number of multiple-choice and essay questions at a certain performance level, you will naturally organize your activities for the day toward accomplishing that objective.

Sub-Goals

The key here is to set many goals on a *frequent* basis. Although passing the bar (with gusto) may be the primary goal, make it more important each day to manage the smaller sub-goals that accumulate into your overall bar preparation. Ideally, every day or week you should have some sub-goal that moves you ever closer to your ultimate goal. One of the problems with the primary goal of bar passage is that it is a delayed goal, making it too easy to put off preparation until tomorrow. Unfortunately, those individual tomorrows have a tendency to build up into a mountain of wasted yesterdays. Furthermore, the goal of bar passage is so challenging that it can at frustrating times seem like a lost cause. Periodic hopeless feelings can be quite demotivating. If instead you focus your efforts on smaller sub-goals that you can attain regularly and frequently, then you create progress to measure yourself against every day and week. Of course, your sub-goals must still be large enough to add up to overall success, but your intent should be to increase the frequency with which you face immediate necessary sub-goals rather than look only to your distant and remote overall goal. If you make consistent progress on these frequent sub-goals, then you also have reason to feel a consistent sense of accomplishment.

Passion

Develop a passion for law. Your licensure will permit you to embark on a long and rewarding career in law practice. Your longevity, success, and satisfaction in that career will depend in large part on how much you care about what you are doing. When others have said that law is a *jealous mistress*, they have meant that law has the capacity to engage you, to attract and absorb your interest, and to satisfy some of your deepest and most profound yearnings, provided that you give law what law is due, which is your undivided attention, indeed your commitment and passion. Many practitioners find that passion for law and then draw on that passion for law throughout their careers. While bar-exam preparation does not offer the full satisfaction of client interaction and advocacy, standing and reputation, authority, and compensation, your bar-exam preparation is nonetheless a once-in-a-lifetime opportunity to court the law itself, to immerse yourself in its power, purpose, and subtle beauty. If the construct helps, then consider bar-exam preparation to be your honeymoon with the law alone before embarking on a long and prosperous marriage.

Effectiveness

While the quantity of your effort in some way counts, do not assume that simply putting in large numbers of hours in bar preparation will lead to success. Don't let your attitude be one of drudgery, like working countless hours deep in a vast salt mine. Instead, ensure the *effectiveness* of your studies. *Productive* hours, not unproductive hours, matter. Volume is not the strategy. Simply sitting in a bar-review course does not count. Mindless activity does not count. Mind*ful* engagement is what matters. Especially avoid the idea that if your studies are consistently easy, then they are effective. The contrary is much more likely true. Think of the last movie or TV show you saw that you felt was educational. Make sure it is a movie or show that you did not take notes on or research further, but it still felt like you learned much, such as a fascinating documentary that you enjoyed. Do you have one in mind? If so, now list all the new things you learned from it. Odds are quite high that the list is very short, somewhat vague, and perhaps disappointing in contrast to what you felt like you have learned. Why did you learn so little despite the fact that it felt so compelling and educational? The answer lies in the difference between *passive* and *active* learning. When you simply watch something, you are being passive and therefore learning little, even if it is interesting and you feel like gains are being made. To retain your newfound knowledge, you must rehearse it and engage in some active behavior.

Effort

You should frequently have the sense of *striving*, of *struggling* even, and then of *grasping* with *special effort*. The performance stars are not the ones who just show up for work each day to once again go through the familiar motions. The stars are the ones who take each day as a mighty struggle to *accomplish* something *new* and *worthwhile*, to break fresh ground with focused effort using just the right angle of the sharpest implement. Although such focused practice is effortful and does not come naturally, there is a huge benefit: not only will your learning sessions be more effective; they will also be more *efficient*. You will learn more in one hour of active practice and rehearsal than in several hours of passive reading or review. Be constantly on the lookout for those tools, practices, and challenges that will *hone* your studies rather than sticking with the blunt tools that simply tread the same old ground. Practice the performance that the bar exam requires. Then make your practice perfect performance. If you are not frequently doing what the bar exam actually requires, and if you are not doing it as well as the bar exam requires, then your preparation will be ineffective. Align your practice to the performance.

Measure

Count, record, measure, and monitor your performance. In order to assess and improve, you need reliable data to guide adjustments. Align these measures with your frequent sub-goals. Using data to make decisions is a key strategy for professionals in many fields. Indeed, data preservation, collection, and use together form the classic assessment strategy. Make and use scorecards. Keep a diary, journal, or log. Count and record anything that might help you improve your exam performance. Do not keep records merely to gloat. Instead, especially record low performances. If you only got half of a multiple-choice bank right, or if you scored fewer than half of the available points on essay questions on a certain subject, then be sure to record those scores. If you failed to practice any questions at all for three days in a row, or if you spent only one or two hours in bar preparation on those days, then be sure to record those low performances. The saying is that *what gets counted gets attention.* Simply by counting and recording performances, you will tend to address your mind and energy to improving those performances.

Assessment

A related strategy that will improve your bar studies is to assess your practices frequently. Lawyers and other professionals are particularly effective at self-assessment. When we are at our best, we are constantly critiquing our own performance and practices. The same should be true of your bar studies. Just because you completed one day or one week of studies that vaguely seemed relatively productive does not mean that you should simply repeat the same activities the next day or week. Ask yourself how you actually used your time, whether you wasted time, and whether you gave your greatest effort. Evaluate your reading comprehension and speed. Confirm that your study locations are promoting your concentration. Assess your study resources and materials. Diagnose your issues and problems, particularly looking for patterns. As you assess, look at how often you are meeting your sub-goals. Also, make projections based on your current performance. If you keep progressing at your current rate, then will you be ready when the day of the exam comes? If your rate of progress falls short, then you need to change your self-study strategies or invest more time. One of the advantages of frequent sub-goals is that you will have frequent opportunities to benchmark your performance gains. Save what works, while jettisoning what doesn't work. Make changes where you see opportunity for improvement. Get different help, try different resources, and change study partners or locations. While you should hold to the tried and true, some of the methods with which you start should probably not be the methods with which you finish. You need not do everything that everyone else is doing or even do everything that your commercial bar-preparation course requires or recommends. Those who retake the bar will tell you that they needed to change their practices. Change your practices *before* taking the bar, not *after* taking the bar.

Improvement

Plan for and expect improvement. Bar preparation is not a matter of proving your intelligence at the first practice attempt. Do not let low scores on your first practices discourage you in your bar preparation. Recognize your performance plasticity. Committed examinees who diligently apply themselves to effective study practices make vast improvements in practice scores leading up to strong bar-exam performance and success. The bar exam is not an intelligence test. It measures your performance at a specific point in time under specific conditions, not your capability to perform. The performance that the bar exam measures is a unique performance, one that if you prepare correctly you may never perform again. Expect low scores on your first practice tests, and expect to improve those scores with diligent and effective practice. Record, compare, and contrast your scores from practice test to practice test. Let your improvement encourage you to increase your studies and confirm the effectiveness of your study methods. Plan for improvement, and work for improvement. Improving is a prime strategy.

Increments

When counting and improving, appreciate the strategic value of thinking about increments. Improvement does not define your full objective. You might improve somewhat, a very little bit, every day that you study and yet not pass the bar. You want to improve *sufficiently to pass the bar*. As you measure and assess your improvement, contrast your gains to what you will need to achieve to pass your state's bar exam. Seventy percent is a common passing score. If you are scoring around fifty percent on your early practice tests and making only small improvements toward sixty percent through the greater part of your bar-exam preparation, then you are not making the incremental gains that you need to pass the bar. *You can only know if you are making adequate progress if you frequently measure and assess your performance.* Without measuring your actual behavior change, you are left with guesses and gut intuition that may not lead to your success. Yes, celebrate your daily and weekly improvement, but at the same time measure the extent of that improvement against your ultimate bar-pass goal. Don't exaggerate the consequence of periodic declines in practice scores. Don't allow a low score here and there to discourage you from consistent effort. Appreciate every gain, no matter how small the increment. Yet be sure that your incremental gains are large enough to reach the goal. You want each sub-goal to be attainable, but you also want the sub-goals to represent meaningful progress. This condition is why it is critical to set many goals and to set them early. The longer you wait, the larger each sub-goal will need to be to stay meaningful and the less attainable they become. An early start will mean an easier life.

Focus

Studying what you do *not* know rather than what you *do* know may sound too simple but is nonetheless an important strategy. Many believe that they are learning best when they feel comfortable and confident about the studied subject. The opposite is truer that learning requires some degree of mental discomfort as the mind forms and adjusts to new cognitive structures. Don't lull yourself into studying only what you already know, even though doing so would feel more comfortable and reassuring. Rather, challenge yourself to study what your practice and assessment shows that you *don't* know. If you are so familiar with a written outline or audio or video recording that you know every word, and getting all of the answers right on your practice tests in one subject area, then force yourself to concentrate on other resources that you don't know so well and to practice tests on which you are not yet performing strongly. Don't waste precious study times making yourself feel good about what you already know. Instead, attack, struggle with, and master what you *don't* know.

Comprehensiveness

To make much the same point in a little different way, you cannot pass the bar examination by performing masterfully on one portion of the exam but abysmally on other portions, having outstanding law knowledge and recall on a few subjects but little or no knowledge on other subjects, or having one or two outstanding skills but little or no skill in other performances that the bar exam requires. Your strategy should be to develop comprehensive knowledge and skill so that you can perform competently on *all* parts and subjects of the bar exam rather than masterfully on a few but poorly on several or many others. You are, in a sense, better off being average everywhere than excellent somewhere while dreadful elsewhere. Scoring consistent sevens and eights on ten-point essays is better than scoring a couple of tens along with a bunch of threes and fours. One very-low essay score, say a one or two out of ten points, pulls down several good scores, turning a bunch of sevens and eights into fives and sixes. Earn points everywhere, not just here and there. Put another way, although lawyers certainly specialize in practice, the profession still generally requires broad basic competence. State bars have determined that lawyers should share a certain quantity of professional knowledge and degree of professional skill. Pursue the strategy of comprehensive preparation rather than piecemeal excellence. You can and will focus your expertise once licensed and in law practice.

Advice

Finally, as a last strategy point, consider a caution about soliciting, receiving, and accepting advice. Don't passively follow the plans, programs, and advice of others without simultaneously judging that those programs and that advice are right for you. Many counselors make for wise decisions but only when you are deliberately thinking, evaluating, discerning, and deciding. Otherwise, blindly following the advice of many others may lead you to adopt programs and practices that do not fit and address your particular needs. Examinees show great variety in their study methods, practices, and resources. What works for one examinee does not necessarily work for another. You may deeply respect, trust, and admire the mentor who gives you bar-exam advice, but your regard for that mentor does not necessarily mean that the advice is for you. You must still make your own determination of your needs based on your superior knowledge of your own current circumstances, capabilities, and preferences. As in so many other endeavors in life, advice may be cheap, wise counsel more costly. Listen more closely to the advice of those who make the bar exam their vocation. Passing the bar exam once does not make that person a bar-exam expert. Studying for the bar exam before even having taken it even less so makes that person an expert. Sure, listen to the counsel of anyone, even those who are studying for the exam right along with you, but rely only on what you independently discern to be trustworthy advice.

2 Health

Health Matters

You should not and in candor cannot abandon your health for whatever period of six, eight, ten, or twelve weeks that you feel you must study intensely for the bar exam. You must at least eat and sleep during your bar studies. That sleep plays an important role in the formation of memories should serve as an extra incentive for attending to your health. You should also give at least some attention to your grooming or other self-care, and also exercise responsibly. Indeed, regular exercise and responsible self-care can promote your bar studies, not just balance them. How you best schedule to satisfy health imperatives while maximizing healthful bar studies will vary widely depending on your personal health and health needs. Draw on what has worked for you in the past while avoiding habits and practices that have not worked. Plan to devote substantial time to studies each day while not attending directly to your health, but also capture small blocks of time between healthy activities.

Accepting

Some people try wait for the perfect opportunity to study. They make sure they set aside an extended period of time when they will be completely undisturbed. They arrange for certain music and other ambient stimulation. These well-intentioned plans can become problematic if you are not careful. The fault with waiting for the perfect study time is that it often turns into an excuse for procrastination. People blame their lack of study on someone or something interrupting them and derailing their progress. While you benefit from making your study time as

17

focused and dedicated as possible, *do not expect perfection*. The real world often denies such ideal conditions, and you should never pass on an opportunity to make even minor progress. Study for 20 minutes immediately after awaking but before cleaning yourself up. Study for another 15 minutes before getting breakfast. Study for another brief period before getting morning exercise. Using meals, exercise, and personal care to pace and space your bar studies can actually improve your study effectiveness as the chapter on Schedule further describes. Set aside dedicated time for study, but also take advantage of those little moments and imperfect conditions.

Adjusting

While you may want and need to make lifestyle adjustments to accommodate your bar studies, don't plan large changes in diet, sleep, or exercise that may disrupt your natural health cycle. Bar studies are a bad time to cut your sleep by half, start a new diet, finally become a vegetarian, or begin training for your first marathon. If you regularly sleep ten hours a night, then you may try cutting back to nine or eight hours during bar studies but not to seven or six hours. If you regularly eat lots of red meat, then maybe eat a little less during bar studies, but don't stop eating meat entirely. If you run regularly, then maybe run a little less but don't entirely quit running. If you ordinarily spend hours every month at the hairdresser, barber, or nail salon, then maybe give those activities a break but don't stop washing and brushing or combing your hair, and cutting your nails. Yes, adjust, but keep the basics in place. You may if you wish make bar studies like boot camp, but then keep in mind that many recruits drop out of boot camp. Dropping out is not an option with bar studies. You will either prepare or not prepare for the bar exam. Adjust enough to improve without abandoning your healthy lifestyle.

Nutrition

If you ever have a time for eating smart, then preparing for the bar exam is that time. Your mind requires nutrition. Much like the response of your muscles with vigorous physical exercise, the harder you use your mind, the stronger it becomes, but also the more and better nutrition it requires. Your diligent studies may tempt you into thinking that you should reward yourself with rich, sugary, starchy, fatty, and fried foods. Don't go that route. Reward your diligent studies with good nutrition, not bad nutrition. You know the difference between brain foods like fish, chicken or other lean proteins, dark fresh fruits and vegetables, and the healthy fats in olive oil, avocados, and nuts, and foods that can interfere with digestion, attention, and concentration like sugary sodas, candy and cakes, and greasy fried foods. Eating healthy can take time and effort. If you do not have skill in food preparation or food shopping and prep time, then seriously consider enlisting family members, friends, or a food service. Eating more fast food should not be an option. Eating more of the healthy home-prepared meals of an understanding spouse, friend, or neighbor may be your best option.

Frame of Mind

The mental state with which you approach your bar preparation may go further toward determining your success than any other factor. Expect to feel overwhelmed, especially initially, with the challenge ahead of you including the hours, days, and weeks of preparation, the large quantity of law that you will memorize, and the practice in which you will engage. The moment you do feel anxious and overwhelmed, though, you should remind yourself of certain truths. First, many others before you have accomplished what you are setting out to do. You probably know several graduates of your law school who passed the bar recently, who for one reason or another you feel are no more capable of passing the bar than you are. If they passed it, then so can you. Keep in mind, too, that you decided to take the bar exam. No one forced you to do so. You decided to challenge yourself with one of the greatest intellectual accomplishments that one can pursue. Next, remind yourself that you cannot prepare for the bar exam all at once. No matter how much preparation lies before you, you can only do one thing at a time, that which is immediately at hand. Thus your real challenge is only to do that which is immediately at hand. Everything else, particularly the accumulation of all of your efforts, must take care of itself. Each time you feel panicky about all that remains to complete your bar preparation, you need only turn back to the immediate task at hand because doing so is all that you can do. In this manner, turn your negative feelings into positive energy. Let the excitement of the bar lead you forward hour by hour, day by day. When you think about it, preparing for a grand challenge like the bar exam is far better than repeating mundane tasks day after day.

Fears

Everyone taking the bar exam has some degree of fear as to the results. You might think that the geniuses among your law school classmates have no fear of not passing the bar. Think again. Higher expectations can create more fear for academic stars than for the average or below-average graduate. In fact, many high performers constantly worry whether they are worthy of their accomplishments, tending to undervalue their obviously significant achievements. Everyone must deal with some degree of fear or anxiety over negative results. You might assume that fear can be useful in spurring preparations, and indeed one way to deal with fear is to get back to studies the moment you sense a rise in your anxiety level, but generally, fear depletes and distracts and is best avoided. If you have an inordinately high level of fear and anxiety that positive action cannot seem to banish, then consider writing down each of your fears with as much specificity as you can muster. Include each negative consequence that you fear would occur if you did not pass the bar exam, things like embarrassment and job loss. Then for each negative consequence, write down the steps you would promptly take to address that consequence, such as in the case of job loss to apply for temporary jobs or return to an old job. The trick is not to eliminate your fears, which would be impossible given the high stakes, but to manage and even harness your fears toward productive actions. Fear is just a feeling, not an inherent characteristic of who you are or a sign of impending doom. Use that fear to motivate you to make plans that will align with your success.

Physical

Your physical health also affects your bar preparation. Illness, injury, or flare-ups of chronic conditions can slow your bar preparation and interfere with your bar-exam performance. You want to remain physically healthy while preparing for the bar exam and arrive at the bar exam in good physical shape. You have some control over those objectives. You can, for instance, schedule your regular physical exam, eye exam, and dental checkup for before your bar-exam preparation begins. Those exams may reveal and address a condition that could have derailed your bar-exam preparation, perhaps fixing a bad tooth or adjusting prescription eyeglasses. Even if those exams simply confirm your good health, you will have gained the peace of mind that your health is as good as you could expect going into bar preparation. If some physical condition begins to arise during bar preparation that suggests an ongoing and worsening problem, particularly infection but also allergies, reactions, and medication imbalances, then address it promptly before it festers into something worse that keeps you from studying. Attend to your physical health. You cannot think clearly through physical pain and cannot perform optimally through physical disability. Don't let poor physical health due to poor health habits limit your bar preparation.

Temperance

Avoid alcohol, marijuana, and recreational drugs. Substances that depress the senses and dull the mind inhibit the transfer of learning from short-term to long-term memory. While your day of studies may have been productive, your mind continues to preserve and process memories throughout the evening. When you imbibe or partake, you impair and impede that processing. Don't undo the good that you have done. Avoid alcohol and drugs not just around study times but even when recovering from studies. Exercise restraint in any other practice that creates risk of injury, illness, or dissipation. If you regularly bungee-jump, skydive, or engage in other extreme sports or recreations, then take a break during bar studies. Bar studies will be vastly more difficult from a hospital bed or in a body cast. If you enjoy mosh pits, mud wrestling, or cage fighting, then plan your next such event for just *after* the bar exam. If you regularly volunteer to fight forest fires or treat Ebola sufferers, then consider delaying your laudable charitable works until after the bar exam. Restrain yourself, cut back, and tone it down. If you must venture boldly out, then wear sunscreen in the desert, watch for sharks in the ocean, stay clear of poisonous snakes in the jungle, and avoid alligators in the swamp and poison ivy in the forests. In all seriousness, arrive at the bar exam intact and healthy. If you absolutely cannot cut out some of your more-adventurous activities in the literal or urban jungle, then at least spread them out. Temper them. The mantra is *moderation in all things.*

Brain Freeze

Despite your best efforts and intentions as to your health, you will find times, perhaps many times, when you feel as if you just cannot learn anything more than you have already learned that day. When you hit the proverbial wall, try briefly doing something different not related to the bar. If you are at an office or library, then just read something mindless or walk around the building for a few minutes before returning to your bar studies. If your brain-freeze state continues when you resume your studies, then put your studies aside. Close your eyes and daydream or even nap. If you still cannot study after that interlude, then consider just waiting it out where you are until your usual time to stop. Brain freeze may tempt you to quit immediately, but if you do so, then you may disappoint and criticize yourself unforgivingly later. Sticking to your study schedule but not absolutely forcing yourself to do unproductive work may give you both the structure and relief that you need. Above all, don't beat yourself up over brain freeze. The point will come when you have exhausted your capacity for the moment. The best thing to do then may be to celebrate that you have stretched yourself so fully. Your ability to concentrate, learn, and improve will return shortly.

Finances

Your financial health remains an important consideration even as you prepare for the bar exam. Keeping your finances in order during bar preparation can go a long way toward giving you the peace of mind to study effectively. Conversely, ignoring your finances can create unnecessary stresses with which you should not be dealing during bar preparation. Put your financial house in order before you begin the dedicated part of your bar preparation. Putting your finances in order does not mean robbing a bank. You will not suddenly find money growing on trees before, during, or after your bar examination. Your net worth may well decline during bar preparation as you forgo earnings, spend savings, and borrow to cover expenses. Indeed, expect your finances to worsen in that one sense of declining net worth, but plan to maintain order in those finances. Estimate and budget for reasonable expenditures, but also control and limit those expenditures where possible. Especially plan to pay essentials like rent, utilities, and insurance, to avoid major disruptions of your bar-exam preparation from loss of or threats to essential services. Don't splurge on unnecessary items simply because you are preparing for the bar exam. Then examine your sources of income including limited earned income but also savings, borrowing from family members, or borrowing from commercial lenders. Ensure that your income from all sources covers your expenditures. Prepay bills, or delegate bill paying to a trusted other, before you begin preparations so that finances do not distract you as you study. Pay enough attention to your financial health during your bar-exam preparation to ensure your peace of mind. When you pass the bar and begin practice, you want to be in the best situation that planning allows.

Commitments

Beyond just your professional and personal goals, you likely have some broader commitments that one could characterize as your central purpose. For some, these commitments are to some core philosophy or set of principles. For others, these commitments represent spiritual connection or religious faith. Regardless of what that central commitment looks like for you personally, you can likely connect that larger purpose to your professional goals, including preparing for the bar exam. Know what gives you a sense of hope, meaning, purpose, trust, and faith, and honor those deeper commitments during your bar-exam preparation. We are not only body and mind but also something deeper or more general akin to spirit. Your body may be in great health, and your mind may be as sharp as the proverbial tack. Yet if your spirit does not have vitality, resilience, equanimity, joy, courage, and other positive attributes, then the bar exam won't build you up and refine you. Instead, it may tear you down and apart, which is not what bar officials intend for you. Get your commitments and spirit right before starting bar-exam preparation, and keep them right during those preparations. Some examinees in retrospect describe the bar exam as a test of faith and find in passing the bar exam proof of their commitments. If the bar exam makes you feel small, then connect yourself with the larger things that you have learned or acquired. The bar exam requires commitment. Show it.

3 Relationships

Relationships Matter

How you relate to others and others relate to you will affect how effectively you prepare for the bar exam. Life goes on while you prepare for the bar, especially for others. While bar preparation will consume your attention, it will not consume the attention of others. You will make changes in your habits and practices while others go on with their ordinary routines. The changes that you make may affect others, sometimes for the better but other times for the worse. Small and large events will arise in the lives of others during your bar-exam preparation just as they do at other times. During your bar-exam preparation, you will have people who are happy with you and people who are not. Relational support, and also conversely relationship stress, affects your mental and physical health while influencing everything you do including sleep, work, studies, productivity, and performance. As at any other time in life, but particularly at this time of bar-exam preparation, you benefit from managing your relationships responsibly and wisely.

Season

The thing about bar-exam preparation, though, is that aspects of your relationships may need to change from their usual. Because bar-exam preparation is typically a once-in-a-career season rather than a regular thing, you must adjust many things in order to set aside the time, energy, and attention that it requires. Relationships are no exception. If you stop doing everything else in order to prepare for the bar exam, then maybe, just maybe, you could maintain your relationships exactly as

25

before and still be effective at preparation. Yet you won't stop doing everything else. You will continue to have at least some responsibilities in other areas, whether family, work, service, other studies, and so on. Relationships is one area in which you should be able to make temporary adjustments while you prepare for the bar exam on the understanding—and the key word here is definitely *understanding*—that after the bar exam the relationships will return to their normal. Explain to your close acquaintances what the bar exam requires and thus what effective preparation requires. Communicate how intensively you will need to study but also be clear as to the date on which your studies will conclude. Make sure that anyone affected by your bar-exam preparation knows that you understand that effect *and* that it is temporary.

Sharing

Share your goal to pass the bar examination, indeed to *shine* on the bar examination, with family members, friends, fellow law students and graduates, employers, co-workers, neighbors, and others who may in some way need to support you or be able to help you. Make a list of anyone you think may need to know, want to know, or be able to help. Divide the list into those persons who might provide study resources, study assistance, financial support, moral support, relief at work, childcare, parent care, or help with household chores or yard maintenance. Add to your list those persons who, while not likely to provide support, should know of your bar studies so as not to expect things of you while you study, particularly in your social, recreational, and charitable circles. Let these persons know that you are getting ready to study intensely for the bar exam, even sending a note card, email, or other message or text to those whom you do not regularly see but who might wonder why they had not heard from you as you study. Invite help where appropriate, even prayer and messages of support. Receiving a meal or supportive message from a friend at just the right moment can lift your spirits and promote your studies.

Family

You cannot and should not abandon your spouse, children, or other family members, or significant other during bar-exam preparation. While you may very well need to adjust and temporarily limit the time that you spend with them, you can and should still plan time together. Make that time together *quality* time. You need to rest your mind and refresh your spirit. When you spend family time, make that time about *them*, not you. They may be curious about your preparation, but probably not. They do not need to hear every little detail. If they do ask, then give a short, positive report before turning the attention back to them and the family activity. Enjoy the activity, and work at helping others enjoy it. Both you and they will feel better if you make the effort to engage with them positively, even if you do not initially feel like doing so. If they express disappointment over your bar-exam preparations (alright, if they *complain*), then resist reacting negatively. If you do react negatively, then everyone will feel worse, you included. Instead, suggest that everyone plan something fun and special for after the bar exam is over. Make those plans, and then keep those plans. You earned it, and *they* earned it.

Children

Consider a few special words about your children. While they will indeed benefit greatly and for a long time from you passing the bar exam, they are less likely to understand and appreciate that future gain than will your older family members. Your parents, siblings, and spouse will get it. Parents and siblings will know that they are about to receive free legal advice for life, and your spouse will have already been online looking at larger homes and resort vacations. Chances are good that some of them won't even miss you while you study for the bar exam. Your children, on the other hand, will wonder where mommy or daddy is all the time. They, at least, will miss you. Make time for children before you make time for anyone else. Keep regular times to spend with your children so that they can look forward to it and rely on it. If you have very young children, then bar-exam preparation is definitely a time to *get help*. Enlist anyone safe, appropriate, and reliable, whether parents, siblings, friends who have their own children, or professional daycare services. Beg, bargain, and pay if you must, but be sure to get help. As every parent knows, the last thing that you can do effectively when caring for young children is concentrate. You can cook, clean, and converse when caring for young children but not study and concentrate.

Other Dependents

Many of us have seasons in life when we are caring for one or more special dependents. That person may be a spouse, child, or elderly parent, perhaps one who has severe disabilities or a severe illness or other temporary, progressive, permanent, or terminal health condition. When a spouse, child, or other family member who lives with you has a major surgery, accident, illness, or other life-impacting event, their sudden need affects you. They may depend entirely, primarily, or at least somewhat on you to care for them directly, transport them for healthcare, or manage their medical, legal, financial, or business affairs. If you know well before the bar exam that you face one or more of those circumstances involving a dependent, then assess with candor whether you should even be attempting the bar exam. If you attempt the bar exam unfairly to yourself *and* your dependent at such a critical time, then you will have done poorly on both counts. You may end up not passing the bar while not caring appropriately for your dependent. In such circumstances, you do not face the proverbial Hobson's choice, where you really have no choice but to proceed in unfair challenge and likely misery. Rather, you have the option of not taking the bar exam until the next administration or later. Be fair to your dependent *and* yourself. If others can temporarily care for the dependent while you complete intensive bar-exam preparation, then you may have found a responsible way forward to the exam. Yet keep in mind that if you have obligations to a dependent that prevent you from preparing for the bar, then you may not yet be ready to obtain a license and practice law until you satisfy your obligation to that dependent. You may have options, such as part-time contract services, to continue your professional development while waiting for a better season to take the bar exam.

Friends

In a way, how you relate to others during your bar studies will reflect how you and your acquaintances value relationship generally. The saying is that *a friend in need is a friend indeed.* During your bar preparation, you are a friend in need. You need the understanding, respect, and support of others. Yet you are also preparing to enter a profession through which you will be especially able to understand, respect, support, and serve others.

You are about to become a friend indeed, an especially knowledgeable and even powerful friend. Most of your acquaintances will recognize that while you need them now, they may need you later. Do not hesitate to communicate both your need now *and* your willingness to help later as soon as you receive your law license. Those who most support you through your bar preparation may well be your first clients and supporters in law practice. Think of bar preparation as another stage in your professional networking. Don't hide that you are preparing for the bar exam. *Advertise* your bar preparation. In doing so, you will be promoting your professional identity and building your professional network.

Fellow Examinees

Unless you are moving clear across the country from your law school right after graduation, you may well be taking the bar exam with at least a few, and possibly many, of your law school classmates. Even if you have *no* classmates taking the bar exam with you, you may still meet some of your fellow examinees, perhaps as you attend commercial bar-preparation-course classes or study at the local law school or law library. Be aware of how your relationship with fellow examinees may be affecting your bar-exam preparation. Some examinees make great study partners, while others do not. You may make a great study partner for a fellow examinee, or you may not. Having at least some contact with fellow examinees is probably wise. They can share resources, schedules, and insight with you, and you with them. You may also get a clearer sense of how your preparation is proceeding, as you hear about their habits, schedules, and practice scores. In keeping in supportive contact, you are also building your future professional network. On the other hand, herd mentality is generally something to avoid, particularly when a challenge as significant as the bar exam is spooking at least some members of the herd. Don't let the stress that other examinees are feeling affect you adversely, especially when that stress is due to negative habits or practices and other distractions that you are not facing. You may do better keeping a little more to yourself during bar-exam preparation.

4 Schedule

Schedule Matters

Bar-exam success requires that you devote substantial time to preparation. Carving substantial time out of your usual or preferred schedule takes planning. Do not simply assume that you will find enough time for bar-exam preparation among your usual or preferred activities. You will not do so. You need more time than small schedule adjustments will allow. While an intense six- to eight-week preparation period just before the bar exam may in many cases suffice, other commitments or circumstances may keep you from fully devoting yourself to such an intensive experience. You may also prefer to avoid the stress of last-minute, intense preparations. Be realistic. Few of us are truly up to such an intense challenge. You may find it far more wise and preferable to plan your bar-exam preparation over a much longer period. Yet if you do so, then do not assume that the longer duration of your preparation will guarantee your success. You must still devote yourself to preparations. Many examinees find that a reasonable mix of long- and short-term schedule strategies providing for both comprehensive and intensive preparation makes the best sense. Consider starting deliberate bar-exam preparation at least six months before the exam, but also arrange at least a month just before the exam when you can devote your full time to preparation. Your long-term comprehensive preparation will ease the anxiety and stress of a last-minute intensive, while you will still have the excitement and gain of at least some intensive preparations shortly before the exam.

Estimating Time

Most of us are poor judges of how much time we need to allocate for major commitments. We tend to be overly optimistic, only to find ourselves short of the necessary hours, days, or weeks we actually need to complete a task. As a result, budgets and timelines often run over our original projections. A few tips can help you overcome such planning errors. First, look backwards for help in crafting your time estimates. Look back at how often you found yourself being interrupted by others. Look at how long it took to complete a task when including the time unplanned obstacles consumed. When we look forward, we tend to picture a future without interruptions and obstacles, but lessons from our past can prove that such problem-free conditions are rare. Include those time-consuming obstacles in your estimate of the overall time commitment. Assume that unintended obstacles will happen again, and have a timeline that can adjust for these challenges to your bar preparation. Another important tip is to create your time estimates based on the individual components of a task, rather than the task as whole. Do not guess at how long it will take to prepare for the bar examination overall, but create estimates for *each part* of your bar preparation. Calculate your final estimate by adding up the time expected for each of the individual elements of a task. Even experts have trouble with this skill. For example, experienced chefs often badly miscalculate how long meal preparations will take, finding themselves scrambling to finish making the food on time. By contrast, when asked to estimate how long each part of the meal will take to prepare and then to add up those individual estimates, they suddenly become accurate at predicting the necessary time. Apply the same logic to your own bar preparation. Estimate each part and total it all up. You may be surprised at how much larger of a time estimate you end up with as compared to your estimate based on the big picture alone.

Devoting Time

You must deliberately identify time to devote to bar-exam preparation. Everyone has a full life. We are all very good at occupying ourselves all of the time. No one has substantial time that they have not already devoted to something else. Yes, some of us have more family, work, or other responsibilities than others of us do, while some have more leisure, vacation, social, or recreational time than others do. Yet all of us fill all of our time, even if that means watching hours and hours of mindless television. Because we all occupy ourselves so constantly with responsibilities and diversions, you nearly must *manufacture* time, *make* time, or *carve* time out of your schedule. Make those schedule arrangements before starting bar-exam preparation. Accumulate and save vacation, sick, and personal days at work for bar studies, if you are working. Recruit family and friends, or trade or hire help, to assume family, household, and other ordinary duties. Suspend your participation in volunteer, social, or recreational activities. In these and other ways, you must deliberately *make* time for bar-exam preparation.

Assessing Time

Saying so may sound strange, but be aware of what you are doing whenever you are doing it. Lawyers and other professionals develop a constant subtle sense of the value of their current activity toward the objective that they are trying to achieve. We constantly measure the worth of what we are doing against the purpose that we have for doing it. If you enjoy aimlessness, then bar preparation is not the time. Indeed, you might want to think of another career outside of law practice if you don't have any particular purpose in life or have a purpose but don't much care about the value of your activity toward accomplishing it. Law practice is generally not as intense and stressful as bar studies are for many examinees. Yet law practice is purposeful. When clients pay you substantial hourly rates for work that you record down to the tenth of each hour, they expect your work to be focused and purposeful. Bar studies are training ground for that purposefulness. Recognize when you are using time well and when you are not. You need not study every minute, but you do need to know generally when you are advancing in your studies and when you are not.

Calendaring

Consider creating an electronic calendar or purchasing a paper calendar solely for your bar-exam preparation. You can, of course, calendar your bar-exam schedule right along with your calendar of other events. Yet at some point as you approach your intensive bar-exam studies, and particularly once you begin those concerted studies, you will want to record detailed day-to-day bar-study plans. Use your calendar to build in frequent sub-goals in advance, adjusting the sub-goals as needed according to the results of your self-measurement and self-assessment. Those detailed bar-exam-preparation plans will clutter and dominate your regular calendar, turning your regular calendar into a project-planning tool that it ordinarily is not. You may find that mixing those bar-study plans with other calendar events that have nothing to do with bar study creates an unhealthy tension and too much distraction in both directions. You may instead want to have two calendars, one for *total bar exam mode* and the other for your normal life. Doing so may help you balance the two lives that you will seem to lead during intensive preparation. You can look at your regular calendar and feel a semblance of normality but then also look at your bar-exam-preparation calendar and feel a sense of total commitment. The main point, though, is to start getting bar-exam-preparation plans in your mind and, better yet, dates on your calendar. Be especially thoughtful and intentional about specific activities on specific dates. Procrastination is not an option.

Accountability

To help meet each of the sub-goals in your calendar, you may want to share it with someone who can hold you accountable. In collaboration with this other person, you should devise positive consequences for meeting each of your milestones and negative consequences for when you don't meet the milestones. Be reasonable and modest in selecting consequences. Remember that you will need to use these consequences frequently to reinforce your frequent sub-goals. Your appointed goal manager should be a person willing and able to follow through with both the pleasant and unpleasant consequences. This role, known as *contingency contracting*, is a big responsibility you are asking the person to take on, so be grateful for the help even if the person is enforcing an unwanted penalty. If you can find the right person to help, then this method may prove to be your greatest ally in managing your time and studies. You won't be the first to have employed this method. Highly skilled and committed professionals, not just bar examinees, rely on contingency contracting to reinforce their preparation for critical performances in different fields.

Stages

You may help yourself by thinking first of the larger stages of bar preparation. To some degree, you will have been planning for the bar exam from as early as your first year in law school and then again in course selection throughout the second year. Yet the first stage of concerted bar-exam preparation often occurs around one year before the bar exam. By that time, you will have chosen and registered for your state's bar exam, applied or begun the application process including the character-and-fitness component, and explored the fields, topics, and subtopics on your state's bar exam. Determine then whether you need to start preparing early (see below), and also set a start date then (also see below). Choose, register for, and pay for a commercial bar-preparation course by then. Get the Multistate Professional Responsibility Exam out of your way at or before this stage, ensuring that you do not take it too early (see a later chapter on this subject). Begin a bar-exam preparation calendar, ensure that you have chosen the right time to take the bar given your other circumstances, and, most of all, ensure that you *want* to take the bar exam and practice law. Your preparations enter a second stage six to eight months before the bar exam when you will need to confirm that each of the above steps are firmly in place. Three to four months before the bar exam, you should have completed all significant administrative steps, made travel arrangements to the bar exam and reserved accommodations, and gotten your health, house, relationships, and finances in order. No later than two months before the exam and possibly significantly earlier you should be immersed in the moment preparing for the bar exam full time, unless you have strong and sound reason to be unusually confident.

Start Date

One of the bigger questions with which bar preppers wrestle is when to start. Setting and planning for a start date is an important strategy. Deciding on a start date enables, indeed forces, you to make necessary study arrangements whether having to do with taking time off from work, obtaining childcare, confirming study location, or collecting study resources and supplies. A start date also helps you begin actual studies rather than putting them off to a later date. The start date that any examinee should select depends on several factors peculiar to the specific bar and examinee. Examinees who have already performed well on standardized tests and in law school and who face a state bar with higher pass rates may reasonably decide that an intense period of four to six weeks would be sufficient. Examinees who do not perform so well on standardized tests, did not get higher grades in law school, and face a state bar with low pass rates should anticipate a longer period of intensive preparation and thus set an earlier start date for intensive studies. Remember that law school grade-point average correlates more strongly with bar-passage rate than other measures like LSAT score or undergraduate grade-point average. Assess your situation frankly. If you had a lower class standing in law school, then plan for longer intensive studies. Consider it again: law school grades are the closest correlation to bar-exam results. If you are in the bottom half or especially the bottom quartile of your class by academic standing, then you likely need to do more preparation, and possibly significantly more preparation, than many or most of your classmates. Your commercial bar-review course may even permit you to attend the prior course so that your final intensive bar-preparation course is actually a review. No one gets a free pass through the bar exam. Everyone must perform. Low class rank does not condemn an examinee or mean a more-arduous bar exam, just as high class rank does not guarantee anything or mean a less-arduous exam. Every administration of the exam results in stories of academic stars not passing while students who barely made it out of law school do pass. Yet that is precisely the point that every examinee needs to take stock and prepare accordingly.

Early Start

On the other hand, start dates, while important as a planning tool to ensure that intensive studies actually begin, can have an adverse effect in putting off useful early preparation. You are, in a sense, preparing for the bar exam throughout law school and even now in reading this book. Examinees often start preparation four, six, eight, or more *months* rather than *weeks* before the bar exam. Early preparation, even for just an hour or two a day, can familiarize you with the materials and habituate you to the process while also eliminating procrastination and relieving stress. Think seriously about an early start, particularly if you

35

discern from your review of your bar exam's content (law fields and topics, addressed in another chapter below) that your law school coursework left large gaps in your bar-exam preparation. From all of your law school courses, make two lists of the courses in which you did well and in which you did poorly. From a third list of your bar exam's subjects, identify any of those subjects that you either did not have in law school or in which you did poorly. Consider those subjects for early studies so that when you reach those same studies in your intensive preparation, you are not seeing those subjects for the first time. Examine your law school performance for deficiency patterns such as in code-based courses, procedure courses, or transactional courses, and then make that deficiency an area for early remediation. Evaluate frankly your test-taking skill. If you perform significantly less well on multiple-choice or essay questions, then consider early practice on that particular skill. Set a start date for intensive bar-exam preparation, but consider starting *now* where you discern that your bar-exam preparation would most benefit. Remediate weaknesses before playing to your strengths.

Intensive Study

Your intensive study in the last two months or so is likely to proceed through stages, too. Follow study schedules recommended by your commercial bar-preparation course unless you are confident that you have a better schedule. Your initial four weeks of intensive study is likely to involve substantial doctrinal review including substantial reading, outline, and flash card work plus substantial instruction whether in class or online, or by other video and audio recording. You should be practicing questions daily at the same time in the numbers and order that your review course recommends. These first four weeks will lay the groundwork for your success. You should remain attentive to your diet, exercise, and rest during this initial intensive period. The next two weeks of your intensive study should involve increased practice exams in larger blocks with more feedback but with continuing substantive development and review. This stage begins to integrate the different bar-tested subjects within each day of your studies and within your practice exams. You should feel your studies gaining momentum during this second intensive stage and should be expending maximum effort. You should also have made all necessary and helpful adjustments by this stage to ensure that your study is the most effective that it can be. You should by the end of this second stage have completed large-block exam simulations that completely familiarize you with exam conditions. Your final two weeks will involve continual all-topics review and may involve a lighter rather than heavier practice-exam schedule, provided that you have completed blocks of questions on all topics. You may feel yourself tapering a little during this final stage to ensure that you are rested but also fresh and familiar with all topics even if practicing questions less often.

Optimizing Time

Still on the subject of time, and strange as saying so may sound, one time can be worth more time than other time. We all have optimum times for study or other activity toward accomplishing our daily objectives. Optimum time is when you are fresh, energized, and focused, ready to perform. Down time is when you are weary, tired, and distracted. Identify your optimum time. Assess when you are feeling most fresh and focused, the times of day when you seem to accomplish the most. Your optimum time may be early morning, mid-morning, mid-day, mid-afternoon, late afternoon, early evening, or late evening, or any combination of those times. Your energy level and ability to concentrate and focus, together with the energy level and activities of those around you, will determine your optimum times. Once you identify those optimum times, *devote them to bar studies*. Protect that time. Be jealous about that time. Draw lines around that time. Guard that time. Expend that time on nothing other than bar studies. Two hours of intense bar studies at your optimum times may be as productive as eight hours of low-energy, distracted studies.

Spacing

We underestimate time's subtlety and complexity, seeing it simply as a straight-line continuum when it instead has other useful features. For instance, we tend to study subjects in blocks, devoting concentrated time to one subject before moving on to the next subject and then the next in linear fashion. By contrast, cognitive studies confirm the greater value of *spacing* the study of a single subject across time rather than concentrating that study into a single time. Block study emphasizes only short-term memory, while spacing study helps move learning from short-term to long-term memory. Studying a subject for a half day but not returning to it again for two weeks can be less effective than breaking the subject into smaller chunks and spacing those chunks out over the same two weeks. When we learn a subject, we hold it in short-term memory. If we do not refresh the subject, then that short-term memory may quickly disappear rather than moving to long-term memory for our later retrieval. Each time we return to a subject that we just learned or began to learn, we are creating and confirming retrieval routes for that learning, essentially moving that learning from short-term memory to long-term memory. Bar exams require that we recall law knowledge, meaning that we must hold that law knowledge in long-term memory. When scheduling your bar studies day to day and week to week, make sure to space your studies across time rather than cram them into single extended times.

Interleaving

Cognitive studies also confirm the greater value of *interleaving* studies, for moving learning from short-term to long-term memory. Again, block practice concentrates the study of a subject into a single time. Block study gives the illusion of mastery and the feeling of flow but without producing reliable long-term memory. Spacing practice across time produces greater transfer of learning from short-term to long-term memory. Yet mixing other subjects, particularly related subjects, into the spaces between times can further increase memory transfer into the long term. Think of *interleaving* as sliding pages of notes on one subject in between the pages of notes on another subject or as *sequencing* your learning one subject right along with your learning another subject. Studies suggest that you learn each subject somewhat slower in this interleaved fashion, as you might expect moving back and forth between subjects, but that you *remember* and *test* better in this on-again, off-again, on-again fashion than with block study. The improvement may have to do with the retrieval and reorganization that occurs each time you return to the subject from other subjects, although cognitive scientists do not all agree on how interleaving works. When planning your schedule, space and interleave, more so than block, studies.

Concentration

Begin by taking breaks for a few minutes each hour of your bar studies. Study for fifty minutes, then take a ten-minute break before beginning with the next hour of study. Move around on your breaks. Don't just noodle around with your smart phone, or if you must, then walk around and swing your free arm while doing so. Stretch, run up and down stairs, snack briefly, or comb your hair or brush your teeth. Do *something* other than stare at a book or computer. Then return to your bar studies refreshed and ready to go for another forty-five to fifty minutes. Gradually, though, include longer study sessions, eventually up to two or three hours. The bar exam includes two-hour to three-hour sessions. You will need to build up the stamina to concentrate for that long of a period. You have probably heard of runners using *interval training* to improve their stamina. As you approach the bar exam, vary the length of your study sessions between shorter bursts of a half hour to an hour, and longer sessions of two to three hours. Although these sessions will tire you, you should nonetheless find your concentration and stamina growing stronger. The point is not to practice comfortably but instead to stretch your capacity. Concentration improves with rigorous practice.

Consistency

Whatever schedule that you plan, stick to it. You never get back the time that you lose. The race goes to the tortoise, not the hare. A little more each day adds up to much more than a lot jammed into a single day. Ten three- to four-hour days of bar study mean much more than one or two twelve-hour or even sixteen-hour days. By keeping to your schedule, you are eliminating the need for catch-up, hurry-up, and makeup days that don't in any case produce the kind of effective learning that you need for bar-exam success. When you do keep to your schedule, you gain a sense of accomplishment, assurance, and satisfaction that fuels you for sticking to your schedule the next day. Success breeds success. At the same time, when you do fall off schedule, brush yourself off and get back on schedule. Expect on one or more occasions to have unavoidable interruptions. Get past the interruption, don't beat yourself up unnecessarily, and then promptly return to schedule. Don't let falling off schedule keep you from trying to catch back up. And when you can't catch back up, don't let it bother you so badly that you give up sticking to the rest of the schedule. Be as consistent as possible.

Phases

The idea that you first learn the law before practicing it may tempt you to spend your early bar preparation solely on reading, reviewing, and otherwise learning substantive law, while putting off taking practice tests and writing practice essays for later, perhaps much later. While you may sense yourself going through phases, and grasping the basic law can certainly help your first performances, do not delay in practicing test taking. You are far better off starting with practice tests a little too early than much too late. We learn better by doing than by simply hearing or seeing. Include in your schedule lots and lots of time for practice tests, particularly where you get feedback that you can use to correct your answers and improve your written work. Don't worry if when taking early practice tests you are getting only half of the answers right. You should quickly begin to improve that early performance. Examinees regularly improve by five, ten, or even twenty percent from one practice test to another. Imagine instead if you had waited until late in preparations to take your first test but scored very poorly on it. Work plenty of practice into your schedule.

Exam Day

Most examinees need to plan at least some travel to reach the site of the bar exam. Plan early for your travel to the bar exam. You may need hotel reservations or even plane or train reservations. Make those reservations early so that you face no added inconvenience over unavailable transportation or accommodations. Planning your travel and accommodations also gives you the opportunity to begin to picture exam day. Don't hesitate in doing so. Envision yourself going calmly through every step that you will take right up until the moment the exam administrator tells everyone to begin the bar exam. Let your mind calmly rehearse the smallest details right down to how you will wake up, dress and ready yourself, check out of the hotel, walk or drive to the exam site, greet other examinees cheerfully, sit at your exam table or desk, and arrange the few things that exam instructions permit you to bring into the exam room. Get those things together now, and practice using them. Familiarize yourself with every detail. These practices will not only calm your fear and anxiety both now and on exam day but will also increase your concentration for the moment that the exam begins. Do not change things on or around exam day. Do not take a sleeping pill the night before if you have never before taken a sleeping pill. One influence on exam performance has to do with whether the physiological functioning you experienced while learning material matches with your physiological functioning while others examine you on that material. The closer the match is between learning and testing conditions, the more likely you'll recall the necessary material. For example, if you didn't learn the material while feeling the groggy aftereffects of a sleeping pill, it is a really poor idea to try taking the bar examination while in a groggy physiological state. You want to feel as closely as possible to how you felt while originally learning the material. If you usually go to bed early, then go to bed early even if you toss around a little or lot more than usual. If you usually go to bed late, then do the same because if you go to bed early you might wake up in the middle of the night. Expect to feel different, but don't do differently. Keep the structure so that change in structure does not add to your natural excitement and stress.

5 Resources

Resources Matter

You are not doing this bar-exam preparation alone. Well, yes, you alone must prepare for you alone to take the exam. No one will be choosing the options and writing the answers with or for you during the bar exam. Yet in gathering professors, instructors, mentors, review books, outlines, video and audio recordings, flashcards, and other resources around you as you prepare for the bar exam, you stand on the shoulders of many who want you to succeed and have worked and will work hard and insightfully to see you do so. Don't ignore the abundant bar-preparation resources. Rather, explore those resources, choosing from among them what you need most at each stage of your bar-exam preparation. Your favorite initial resources may be review books and video and audio lectures, but you will soon be gathering and creating outlines and employing flash cards, and then you will feel strong need for practice questions with clear feedback. You may find particular bar-preparation instructors especially helpful at times but then may seek a former professor's clarification and end up drawing on a bar mentor. Don't be proud of your own insight. Investigate every potential resource as you discover it, and then choose, deploy, and value those resources that mean the most to you at each stage of your preparation.

Law School

As bar examinations have grown more difficult and pass rates have declined, more law schools have offered third-year and last-term bar-preparation courses as an endpoint to their curriculum. The first-year law school curriculum tends to be heavy on the core doctrinal subjects that the Multistate Bar Examination tests. Save your outlines from those courses, and keep in contact with your most-helpful first-year professors. The second-year curriculum tends to offer additional doctrinal courses that the Multistate Essay Examination or state-specific essay questions test, mixed with skills courses and specialty electives. If your law school does not require that you take Negotiable Instruments, Secured Transactions, Sales, or other bar-tested subjects, then consider taking those courses as electives. Again, save outlines and foster contacts. The third-year curriculum tends to be more experiential and integrative. This progression means that many graduates will not have studied core bar-tested subjects for two-plus years. Hence the addition of third-year and last-term bar-preparation courses. *Take full advantage of those courses.* Third-year law school bar-preparation courses are not a panacea for an instructional program weak on doctrinal studies of bar-tested subjects. Yet they can help lay important groundwork for further bar preparation. Consider taking as many bar-preparation courses as your law school offers. Check with your law school, but schools studying graduate pass rates may report that graduates taking those courses pass the bar exam at significantly higher rates.

Commercial Courses

Take a commercial bar-preparation course, no matter how confident you are of your ability to study for the bar exam on your own. From your first day of law school, plan for meeting commercial bar-preparation-course expense. Ensure that you have the savings or are able to borrow the cost. If you are confident of which bar exam you will take and what provider offers the best course for that bar exam fitting your study schedule and preferences, then consider registering early for a course at discounted price. Yes, commercial courses can be expensive, and no, you don't have to take the most-expensive course, but take a reliable course. Determine reliability first by investigating online the course's program, resources, and reputation before committing. Ensure that the course provides state-specific materials for your state's bar exam. Ensure that the course offers classroom instruction if you prefer it to online instruction and the daytime or nighttime instruction that you prefer if instruction is synchronous rather than asynchronous. Ask your law school's bar-exam director or academic-resource coordinator about the strengths, weaknesses, and reputations of different commercial courses. With your law school's help, find a recent-graduate bar-exam mentor, and ask that mentor about the best courses. Graduates studying for the bar exam share their study experiences with other graduates. After they pass the bar exam, they can often share sound and timely advice on preferred courses. Decide whether you should take any of the supplemental courses that commercial courses offer as add on. If you discern that you should start early on bar-exam preparation, then consider selecting a commercial course that will allow you to take the course *twice* before the bar exam, once while you are still in law school and once after you graduate and immediately before the bar exam.

Outlines

Outlines, meaning concise summaries of the law, are a significant tool when you form and use them properly. Making the perfect outline is not sufficient to prepare for the bar exam. You may know your outline inside and out, upside and down, but still not have the fluency to recall law or the skill to apply it. One part of the outline triggers another so that with concerted study you could reproduce 90% of the whole thing but still not spot the important issues in a fact pattern or analyze those facts using the law. Fact patterns must trigger law recall and application, not outline dumping. Outlines are simply a way to ensure that you know law, not that you can recall and use it where you need to do so on a bar exam. That said, developing a detailed, diagrammatic, mnemonic-laden, one-page outline for each of the seven Multistate Bar Examination subjects and each of the eight or so additional subjects that your state bar will test can be a useful way of confirming and rehearsing your knowledge. The advantage of a total 15 or so pages of attack outlines is that you can review the whole outline the mornings of the bar exam, at lunch hours, and again in the evening before the next day's bar.

Flashcards

You may wonder what advantage flashcards can have over a reliable outline. While the outline and flashcards should reflect the same substantive law, flashcards add several advantages. First, while one side of the flashcard would include the same

44

substantive law appearing in an outline, the card's reverse side should carry a brief trigger with which to associate that substantive law. The triggers could be single law terms or short law phrases to define, or they could be brief fact patterns or procedural context. By breaking the terms you need to know into individual components, you can more easily practice those components and spend extra time rehearsing any troublesome terms or phrases. Flashcards also make it easier to precisely measure and assess your progress by counting the average number of cards you got right and wrong during timed daily trials. Watching your performance improve from seven correct per minute to fifteen correct per minute to thirty-three correct per minute can be an additional source of motivation and feedback on the quality of your study techniques. Another advantage is that single cards isolate the law that you must recall from other information that might be serving as supportive context. The bar exam requires that you recall specific isolated laws and rules. Flashcards, shuffled and used in active, game-like fashion, can increase the speed, fluency, and accuracy of your recall on any law topic, in random order just as the bar exam works. When you study using only an outline, you might unintentionally find yourself dependent on the particular sequence of facts, much like recalling the alphabet or lyrics to a song tends to be easier and faster when you follow the familiar sequence. Because the bar exam presents law concepts in random order and you are under considerable time pressure, you must quickly and accurately recall rules outside of any particular sequence. Another hidden risk of outlines is that you may trick yourself into thinking you know the rules better than you really do. When you can see the trigger and the answer at the same time, you may falsely believe that you would have been able to readily state that answer without seeing it next to the trigger. Flashcards force you to commit to saying the answer in the presence of the trigger alone. In fact, research suggests that you should actually say the answer aloud before flipping the card to see your feedback. Thinking the answer silently to yourself is less effective, while just passively staring at your cards without an active response on your part is meaningless. One of the most consistent findings from research on how people learn is that active practice is significantly more valuable than passive exposure. When you use flashcards correctly, they make learning an active experience. Some self-discipline is necessary because flashcards can become passive unless you force yourself to respond actively. You can purchase cards, create your own, share sets with others, or create them using online apps for viewing on your computer, reader, or smartphone. Consider adding flashcards as a helpful resource.

Classroom Instruction

Some law schools and commercial courses offer live classroom instruction for bar preparation. Live instruction has its advantages. Instructors who know the bar-exam format, know the law, and can teach the skills that the bar exam requires, can help you improve your performance. Highly experienced and wise bar-exam instructors can have a way of conveying insight and confidence that written materials cannot convey. While for content you may do just as well with recorded lectures, live instruction enables you to draw on the instructor's expertise beyond what the instructor planned to share in lecture. You may be able to question the instructor on confusing law points, gain tips on bar-exam skills, and meet with the instructor before or after class or on class breaks to locate resources, clarify law, and (most importantly) get help diagnosing problems with your performance or preparation. Some examinees may hold themselves more accountable to live instructors than to promulgated schedules.

Video Recordings

Video lectures are popular resources that commercial bar-prep services use frequently. Advantages of video lectures over classroom lectures are the asynchronous, time-shifting flexibility they afford and the commute time they save getting to and from the classroom. Disadvantages include the lack of interaction with the speaker such as the ability to ask questions and gain clarification, and the lack of support and stimuli from other students in the classroom. As such, video recordings tend to become very passive experiences, especially since we are accustomed to being passive as we watch screens. Fill-in-the-blank exercises that some bar-preparation courses use, and other exercises while listening to or immediately after concluding segments of video recordings, can increase your concentration and engagement. The quality of video lectures can also vary widely.

Some show only the speaker without other supporting visuals. Others include both the speaker and slide shows or other visual materials supporting the speaker's presentation. Others show only the visual materials without showing the speaker, the speaker's voice instead just playing over the slides, pen-casts, or other visual materials.

Audio Recordings

An advantage of audio recordings over video recordings is that you can listen while driving or doing some other things, like watching children or doing housework, that while requiring your visual attention do not require concentrated thought. Listening to an audio recording on a subject as you drive home from a classroom lecture on that subject can repeat and reinforce learning, helping you move that learning from short-term to long-term memory. Use headphones or earbuds to listen to audio recordings while riding the bus, watching your children at the playground, or otherwise fitting in some study while out in public. Audio recordings can be a helpful supplemental resource. Do not, though, overestimate their value. Lulling yourself to sleep at night playing audio recordings of bar-preparation lectures is a very poor practice. A disadvantage of audio recordings is that unless you are simultaneously reviewing a programmed workbook or otherwise using a coordinated resource, you are not getting the visual stimuli and active engagement that increases your uptake, understanding, organization, and recall. Audio recordings should not be your primary resource.

Practice Questions

Quality practice questions, either released questions from past multistate bar exams or exams in your state, or carefully crafted questions patterned after actual questions, or both, are critical resources for your bar preparation. The quality of the multiple-choice and essay questions that you practice, and particularly their alignment to the question forms that your state's bar will use, is important because the learning strategy is to practice the actual performance, not something else that poorly approximates the actual performance. To develop skill, you need to practice questions like the ones that you will face on the bar exam. For example, as the chapter on multiple-choice questions further details, the psychometrics experts at the National Conference of Bar Examiners have developed and shared strict guidelines for the design, form, and content of the Multistate Bar Examination's multiple-choice questions. You should be practicing questions of that design, not some other design. The significant frustration of poor practice performance may be due to poor construction of practice questions. Ensure that you have quality practice questions available to you as a consistent resource. The National Conference of Bar Examiners offers online examples of multiple-choice and essay exams, and performance tests, and for a fee provides practice questions with model answers and explanations. These resources would obviously be the most reliable for bar exams using the Conference's examinations.

Feedback

One of your greatest resources is to arrange for an online grading service or other feedback on both your practice multiple-choice performance and especially on your essay practice. You should not be simply practicing multiple-choice questions, looking at your score, and hoping to do better next time. Instead, you should be reviewing explanations both for your correct answers because you may have guessed or used an incorrect rationale and for your wrong answers to correct your answer and rationale. Practicing is alone not enough. You need to practice and then evaluate your practice. You need to learn from both your correct and your wrong or incomplete answers. You can only do so when you are discerning the law, rule, or rationale that supports the correct and complete answer. You may be able to decipher that rationale using only the question and your outline or other substantive-law materials, but here detailed answer explanations or, in the case of essay questions, model answers are a hugely valuable resource. Make sure that you have that resource available to you. Online commercial service is available to score and analyze your practice bar-exam essay answers. You should also be getting individual feedback on your practice essay answers from a rigorous reviewer, who has your best interests at heart, or at least comparing your answer to a model answer and scoring rubric. Enlisting the help of a competent and caring peer can be enormously beneficial. That peer could practice your flashcards with you, forcing you to measure your progress and make active responses for evaluation. See the chapters below on practice and on multiple-choice and essay questions for more detail regarding practice evaluation and using feedback.

Mentors

An earlier section in this chapter mentions locating a recent-graduate bar-exam mentor. Stay in touch with the law school acquaintances you made who were senior to your own class, as they take and pass the bar. Be deliberate about seeking their advice. *Everyone* who passes the bar exam will have at least *some* advice if for no other reason than to get to speak with elation about having the bar exam behind them. While you need to chart your own path, the paths that others followed can give you clear clues about the direction most fitting for you. Do not overlook your law professors as mentors. They will have guided and supported dozens of graduates through bar-exam preparation and collected much wisdom around that preparation. They may also know you well enough to give especially effective counsel. Some commercial bar-preparation courses assign an attorney mentor to review your online performance, contact you periodically with guidance or encouragement, and be available for consultation. While you may also get bar-exam advice from lawyers, particularly if you are still clerking at a law firm while beginning your bar-exam preparation, be cautious in accepting advice from lawyers who took a different-format bar exam many years ago. Bar exams, pass rates, bar-preparation resources, technology aids, learning theory, *and* the law have all changed a lot in the past decade or two and will continue to change.

6 Content

Content Matters

Knowing the content of your bar exam, meaning the law that the exam actually tests, is critical to your preparation. Law is vast. Fortunately, the bar exam tests only a slice of that vast amount of law. Even more fortunately, bar examiners disclose in advance the subject areas that they will test. Not only do they disclose the law fields that will be on the exam, but for certain tests, in particular the Multistate Bar Examination used in nearly every state and Multistate Essay Examination used in about half of the states, they also disclose the testable topics and subtopics within those fields. Only a fool or glutton for punishment would disregard these disclosures and attempt to study all fields and all topics within those fields. Beyond the advantage of disclosure of fields, topics, and subtopics, you may also locate resources, particularly but not exclusively commercial bar-preparation-course resources, that summarize topic-testing patterns. For instance, to teach my law school's free state-specific bar-preparation essay workshop, I study and summarize the testing pattern of my subject for the past ten-plus years. You can thus see how knowing the fields and their topics and subtopics, and then adding to it some sense of the most-frequently tested topics within fields, can give you both confidence and a genuine advantage. Research field, topic, and subtopic coverage as you prepare for the bar exam.

MBE Subjects

Nearly all bar exams include the Multistate Bar Examination, a 200-question multiple-choice test scoring 190 of the 200 questions.

Study the Multistate Bar Examination subjects. The Multistate Bar Examination portion of the bar exam is the same in every state. The Multistate Bar Examination tests the seven subjects of civil procedure, constitutional law, contracts, criminal law and procedure, evidence, real property, and torts. Plan early to do well on these subjects. Take these courses in law school whether or not your curriculum requires that you do so. Learning a subject in a short bar-review course just before the bar exam is not ideal. Refreshing yourself on a subject that you have already learned in a law school course is far better. The National Conference of Bar Examiners drafts the Multistate Bar Examination. Its website provides a five-page outline showing the tested topics and sub-topics in each of the seven subject areas. The five-page outline also indicates the proportion of questions asked on various topics. Examining the outline should convince you of the need to study these topics while also serving as a focus, reminder, and guide during your studies.

MEE Subjects

About half of state bar exams include the Multistate Essay Examination. If you are taking the bar in one of those states, then study the additional Multistate Essay Examination subjects. The National Conference of Bar Examiners drafts the Multistate Essay Examination, as it does the Multistate Bar Examination. The Multistate Essay Examination includes the same seven subjects as the multiple-choice format Multistate Bar Examination but then adds the subjects of business associations, conflict of laws, family law, trusts and estates, and secured transactions. Once again, plan early to prepare for these subjects. While the Multistate Bar Examination subjects are required courses at many law schools, the additional Multistate Essay Examination subjects are much less likely to be so. If your state bar administers the Multistate Essay Examination, then take these additional subjects as elective courses. The National Conference of Bar Examiners website provides an outline showing the topics and sub-topics within these subjects. Use that outline to ensure that your studies are preparing you to do well on those subjects.

State-Specific Subjects

Determine any other subjects that your state bar tests if it uses any test other than the Multistate Bar Examination and Multistate Essay Examination. About half of state bars, those not adopting the Multistate Essay Examination, draft and include essay questions testing your knowledge of specific state law. Those state-specific essay questions will test some or all of the seven Multistate Bar Examination subjects but may also test several subjects that are not on the Multistate Bar Examination. Those extra state-specific subjects commonly include corporations, professional responsibility, remedies, and wills but may also include unusual subjects like community property or statutory schemes like motor-vehicle no-fault law and worker's compensation law. Preparing for the Multistate Bar Examination alone is not preparing for the bar exam. Your performance on the Multistate Bar Examination may represent only half or less of your score. Be sure that you know all of the subjects that your state's bar exam will test, and then prepare early, late, and in-between for all of those subjects.

Required Score

Learn how your state's bar examiners will score your bar exam. Scoring practices including the weight given to each section and minimum passing scores vary from state to state, particularly within states that do not follow Uniform Bar Examination format. The National Conference of Bar Examiners maintains individual state scoring information on its website, which would also be available directly from the state's bar examiners. While you expect to perform at your best no matter how the examiners score your effort, scoring can matter in how you allocate your preparation time and effort. As indicated elsewhere in this book, the bar exam tends to reward comprehensive rather than peculiar performance. Although you may be able to do so, you should not generally *plan* to overcome poor performance on one section with stellar performance on another. Instead, plan to perform with at least minimal competence on all parts of the exam, even if your state bar weights all parts of the exam equally. You may feel that the strength of your skill in one area will offset weakness in another, but you may instead find that remediating the weakness with a little more bar preparation pays greater scoring dividends than honing your strength. After all, low scores leave more room for improvement than do high scores. Olympic performers can only achieve tiny gains no matter how hard or long they struggle because they are already near optimal athletic performance. In the same way, given that you have only limited time, you don't want to invest all your efforts into achieving a tiny gain in one area that will have an inconsequential effect on your overall performance. For the same investment of time and energy, you may have a huge leap in overall ability if you focus on your weak spots. You always want to find the areas that offer you the greatest potential for improving performance. The incremental gain that your studies achieve may be greater in your poorer performance areas than in your better areas. Moreover, a few state bars require that you reach a minimum score in one or more parts of the bar exam no matter how high the rest of your bar-exam score is. If you do decide to ignore a difficult area of the law that you just cannot seem to master after at least some diligent study, then be sure that it is a *very small* subtopic that you are ignoring, one unlikely to be on the exam.

Scaling

Do not worry unduly about your bar exam being especially difficult compared to prior exams. The National Conference of Bar Examiners *scales* Multistate Bar Examination scores. The examiners add a certain number of points, usually in the range of 10 to 15 points, to your raw score in order to equate the exam's difficulty to the difficulty of prior exams. If your exam turned out to be more difficult than prior exams, then you will receive additional scaled points to ensure that the exam's difficulty does not affect your results. If your raw scores on practice exams are just below your state's required passing score, then scaling may help you pass. Scaling improves your Multistate Bar Examination raw score, although you will not know until after the exam by how much. Read more about scaling on the National Conference of Bar Examiners website. While the National Conference of Bar Examiners scales the Multistate Bar Examination, state bars may or may not scale scores on their state-specific essay or performance tests. Investigate your state bar examiners' scaling and scoring practices until you know approximately what score you must obtain for your practice and assessment purposes, and are confident that the examiners will treat you fairly.

Scoring Practices

Some state bar's examiners disclose additional information in the guise of guidelines or *comments* on how they will score essay or performance answers. Investigate your state bar for those guidelines. You may find that the examiners expressly value answers that read like an experienced lawyer's work. Their guidelines may be to use only the given facts unless directed to draw inferences, and to follow each instruction closely. The examiners may tell you to organize arguments in logical sequence before writing, to discuss both sides of any issue that may have two sides, and to discuss all material issues even if your resolution of a prior issue would appear to preclude consideration of later issues. The guidelines may caution you to answer *every part* of each question. If your state bar's examiners do disclose guidelines, then you will probably find those guidelines to reflect practices with which you are already fully familiar and in which you are already well versed. Read and plan to follow the guidelines anyway. Although you may already know and for the most part follow those practices, you may not appreciate the emphasis that the examiners give them in scoring. If the guidelines say to use headings and paragraph breaks to help reflect the structure and organization of your answer, while avoiding stream-of-consciousness writing, then use headings and paragraph breaks, and avoid stream-of-consciousness writing, as if your bar passage depends on it. Your bar passage may indeed depend on it.

Conduct Rules

While licensure generally requires passing the Multistate Professional Responsibility Examination, that test is not part of the bar exam. The National Conference of Bar Examiners drafts the Multistate Professional Responsibility Examination, just as it does the Multistate Bar Examination and Multistate Essay Examination. While state bars require that you pass the Multistate Professional Responsibility Examination, you must take the exam at some time other than during the bar exam. You may wish to take the Multistate Professional Responsibility Examination just after you complete your law school course or program in professional responsibility, when the conduct rules will be most familiar to you. The National Conference of Bar Examiners offers the

Multistate Professional Responsibility Examination four times each year at many more sites than the typically single-state-site bar exam. Before taking the Multistate Professional Responsibility Examination, determine how long your state bar will let you retain and use a passing score. State bars vary on how recent your passing score must be. Don't take the exam too early, or you may lose your passing score.

Knowledge Level

Every examinee understands that to perform well on the bar exam, you need a certain minimum level of knowledge. What you might not appreciate is that some evidence suggests that reaching a much higher level of knowledge than the minimum that the bar exam requires does not necessarily give you an advantage. Bar examiners possess a requisite level of knowledge. They also expect examinees, most of whom are very recent law school graduates, to possess a certain level of knowledge, certainly one that demonstrate competence but not necessarily one that demonstrates deep subject mastery. The questions are, after all, fairly rudimentary in their nature simply because of the bar exam's limited time and restrictive format. Examiners can't do too much with a multiple-choice question or even, for that matter, with an essay question, given the time and format limitations, not to mention the limitations imposed by relatively objective evaluation and scoring. Given these time-and-format limitations and the examiners' tempered expectations, you may find yourself doing better on practice questions in areas where your level of knowledge is good but not necessarily outstanding, masterful, or excellent. You may, in other words, not be doing yourself any favors by applying the superior knowledge that you have in one or more topics or subtopics, gained for instance through a research paper, teaching-assistant role, or clerkship. Sometimes you need to fly at 1,000 feet rather than 100 feet, meaning that sometimes you need to think at a lower level than at the highest level of which you are capable. Some things you need to simplify and clarify, even while you hope to demonstrate your overall mastery of any subject. You can know too much, just as you can know too little. Next consider some special problems that the Multistate Bar Examination subjects present.

Civil Procedure

Procedure questions present two distinct challenges when compared to substantive-law (doctrinal) questions. First, procedure questions are sometimes interwoven with doctrinal questions, making issue spotting more complex. Second, the procedural issues may be harder to identify. With substantive-law questions, rights, charges, claims, and defenses are the core issues. You must be sure that you know the law, meaning the concepts, rules, elements, conditions, and definitions. Thus, doctrinal subjects often lend themselves well to orderly outlines where one law construct bears clear relationship to other law constructs, so that your law knowledge builds from one concept to another. If you can recall a little, you can often recall a lot. By contrast, civil-procedure questions tend to present problems in the context of the adversary system, where the parties and court are required to react to strategies as they unfold. Civil procedure's content structure involves process knowledge—actions, reactions, and decision standards—rather than a hierarchical outline of descending claims. You must recall rules, procedures, and standards associated with interests, objectives, actions, options, responses, and decisions. You must also be sure that you understand the parties' competing strategic interests. The three major topics of *personal jurisdiction, subject-matter jurisdiction,* and *venue* are examples. While you must know the rules, standards, and definitions associated with each of those topics, the jurisdiction and venue issues will arise when a party with one set of interests and objectives strategically sues another party in a certain court and location, to which the second party must respond, perhaps requiring a court's ruling. Whatever procedural rules you apply, perhaps involving pleading, joinder, discovery, summary judgment, trial, post-trial proceedings, or appeal, you must do so cognizant of the parties' interests and options, and the standards the law requires the court to apply. In some cases, particularly where summary judgment is involved, you will have to layer this process knowledge onto your doctrinal knowledge in order to write a first-class answer.

Contracts

Contract questions tend to have a lot of facts, such as a series of written or oral communications, dates, quantities, terms, and conditions. While contract-formation law (offer, acceptance, and consideration) is relatively straightforward, examiners tend to give you more facts in order to reach and test that law. Fact patterns grow even longer and more complex when they involve employees or agents acting for a corporate party or the interests of third-party beneficiaries. Complex fact patterns require more time and effort. You have to get the facts straight. They also invite error. Reading the question's call before reading the full fact pattern can help you extract and organize relevant facts. Quickly outlining the facts or drawing a picture of them is another tactic. Contracts questions can also lend themselves readily to multiple sub-parts or to a final twist or turn as to the outcome. This characteristic means you can be forming ideas as you read the question, only to find by the end of the question that the examiner wants you to think about something else altogether. This feature is another that reason reading the call of the question first is a good idea. Know the law, but be sure to read and understand the facts, just as much in contracts questions as elsewhere. As to the law itself, contracts law has an overarching order to it involving which law applies, U.C.C. or common law, and then whether the parties formed a contract, breached the contract, have defenses, and should have certain remedies for breach. The question of contract formation also has an overarching order to it involving offer, acceptance, consideration, and terms. These larger frameworks remain important even if your sharply analytic mind wants to seize upon one of contract law's many minor rules and address only that rule. Be cautious of falling into the trap of deciding or addressing a question on a subsidiary contracts rule when following the framework may show you other more-important issues. See your state bar exam's topic and subtopic outline for more detail.

Constitutional Law

Constitutional law has a unique content structure that requires an exam approach unlike other subjects. Constitutional-law questions are uniformly *whether a certain action is constitutional.* Making that analysis often requires two steps, first to determine whether the government had the power to take the questioned action and second whether the Constitution limits that power. So for example, acts of Congress must fall within Congress's enumerated powers, while acts of the President must fall within the President's enumerated powers or powers appropriately delegated by Congress. States retain expansive police powers. Limits on these powers include the many individual rights guaranteed in the Bill of Rights, some rights that the Constitution does not enumerate, and more generally what due process or equal protection require. Questions often require that you also recognize and address an underlying federalism or separation of powers issue, which likewise limits government's authority. While these constructs depend on clauses within the Constitution and its amendments, you must very often recall and apply the Supreme Court's standard or multi-part test for that constitutional construct. Recognizing the specific constitutional issue, recalling the specific provision and associated Supreme Court test, and analyzing any associated due process or equal protection issues do not complete your challenge, though. The actors and actions themselves vary widely. A constitutional-law fact pattern may involve the President exercising war, appointment, or veto powers, Congress authorizing federal regulation of commerce, a federal agency promulgating those regulations, a state legislature enacting legislation affecting interstate commerce, a state agency regulating speech or association, or a private person or entity acting in violation of law, rule, or regulation. You must have not only clear knowledge of the basic constitutional-law constructs but also fluency in their application, a process that one scholar likens to peeling an onion very quickly so as to avoid painful tearing. Prepare earnestly to develop that fluency and facility. See your state bar exam's topic and subtopic outline for more detail.

Criminal Law and Procedure

Criminal-law questions may reproduce verbatim or paraphrase or summarize in brief all or portions of the statute that you must apply to determine whether the suspect has committed a crime. In that respect, criminal-law questions can involve relatively routine and straight-forward application of black-letter law to clear and often compelling facts. In doing so, you may well have to recall and apply key common-law or criminal-code definitions for traditional terms of art, adding a manageable challenge. Applicability of certain defenses to specific crimes is also a popular but manageable test subject. Yet the special challenge that criminal-law questions often present has to do with the suspect's state of mind. You must often read the presented statute or summary very carefully to discern the wrongdoer's state of mind that the statute requires for conviction while also reading and construing the scant facts very carefully for evidence of that state of mind. The examiner may use any element of the charge, such as entry or possession, to test your treatment of a boundary or close-call issue, but state of mind presents its own peculiar examination opportunity and problem. Criminal-procedure questions are, by contrast, usually narrow but subtle tests of constitutional-law constructs like *reasonable expectation of privacy* or *probable cause* in the context of search or arrest, or *custodial interrogation* in the context of Miranda warning. You often must know and recall the Supreme Court's latest iteration of these and other constitutional issues around individual rights of the criminally charged defendant. Pay particular attention to recent Supreme Court decisions and hot topics relating to criminal procedure. See your state bar exam's topic and subtopic outline for more detail.

Evidence

Among all bar-tested subjects, evidence questions may be the most discrete, peculiar, and isolated from other subjects, a quality that can surprise and mislead examinees. You may feel that evidence relates closely to civil procedure and criminal procedure, and even to criminal law, torts, contracts, property, and any other subject frequently involving litigation. Yet while other subjects may often implicate the existence or sufficiency of evidence, with the exception of criminal procedure they do not typically address the *admissibility* of that evidence, which is the core evidence subject. Criminal procedure considers admissibility in its own peculiar context of constitutional rights and protections, such as the confrontation clause, privilege against self-incrimination, or the exclusionary rule for evidence obtained in violation of Fourth Amendment rights. Evidence, though, has its own complex set of rules. The fact patterns in evidence questions are often short. Your challenge lays not so much in reconstructing the parties' strategic interests, which are instead often obvious. The party offering the evidence wants it in, while the objecting party wants it out. You must, though, recognize that parties may offer evidence for two or more different purposes, such as either to prove character consistent with conduct, on the one hand, or to attack credibility, on the other hand. Examiners often require that you distinguish the specific purpose for which the proponent offers the evidence. As this point suggests, your major challenge is in the evidence rules themselves, which often require that you analyze quickly and clearly several layered issues. Relevance and undue prejudice, requiring discerning probative value and effect, are often major issues but only among several other major issues. You may need to proceed promptly to hearsay or privilege issues. You may also need to conclude with an analysis of witness foundation, document authentication, or the best-evidence rule. These features of evidence questions make skill at issue spotting, accuracy of rule recall, facility in rule application, and fluency in written analysis all key evidence-question skills. Most of all, you need precise knowledge of the rules. Examiners often test not the major rule but its minor exception or peculiar balancing test. To simplify the considerable issue-spotting challenges, consider focusing first on *what* the proponent offers, meaning whether testimony, tangible evidence (an exhibit to authenticate), or demonstrative evidence. If testimony, then consider whether the testimony describes what the witness *saw* (foundation issues around personal knowledge), *heard* (hearsay issues), *happened in the past* (character evidence), or *reviewed* (expert testimony). See your state bar exam's topic and subtopic outline for more detail.

Property Law

Complex fact patterns with multiple parties, transactions, events, and dates are a primary challenge of property-law questions. Be sure to take the extra bit of time to note and even chart those facts to get them straight. You may know and even like the extraordinary technical clarity of property law, but if you consistently get the facts wrong, you will lose considerable points. At the same time, property law is itself complex and even foreign enough to present recall and fluency challenges for many examinees. The various joint, present, and future interests of property owners, the rights of others arising by covenant, use, or zoning, peculiar concerns over conveying real property, mortgaging real property, and ways in which property law treats title transfer and recording, are all technical issues with which examinees may have no practical or clinical experience and thus be relying solely on classroom instruction. In its Rule Against Perpetuities and associated treatment of future interests, property law also includes difficult is-it-worth-it subtopics with which many examinees struggle. You are not alone if you find future interests a special challenge. These challenges make practicing property-law questions a particularly important preparation strategy. You may love property law, or you may not, but in either case, put in the practice. See your state bar exam's topic and subtopic outline for more detail.

Torts

The subject of torts has a straight-forward content structure often making it a favorite of examinees. You must generally recall and name the claim, recall the claim's elements or, if it doesn't have elements, then its definition or conditions, and then apply that law to the facts. You may then need to consider any defenses. Torts can present a moderate challenge in recalling the many claims and their elements. Invasion of privacy, for example, may come in any one of the four different forms of intrusion, appropriation, public disclosure, and false light, depending on the jurisdiction. The numerous elements of misrepresentation (a false material representation made knowingly to induce reliance causing loss) and, separately, defamation (false words published of and concerning the plaintiff that together with extrinsic facts lower the plaintiff's reputation causing special damages other than in the case of an exception to special damages) are each fairly subtle and grossly overlap, making them read more like meandering definitions. Yet while recalling claims and elements presents a straightforward if moderate challenge, the greater challenge can be in the examiner's decision to test any number of special torts rules. Those rules can include subtopics like: the First Amendment's effect on defamation of public officials and figures adding an actual-malice element; the expert-witness requirement to establish the professional's standard of care in malpractice cases other than for obvious malpractice; and the three forms of design, manufacturing, and warning defect in products-liability cases, and the seven factors of the Second Restatement's risk-utility test to determine when a product is in a defective condition unreasonably dangerous. While considering torts a straightforward and manageable subject, do not underestimate its subtlety and complexity. See your state bar exam's topic and subtopic outline for more detail. Next consider some special problems that the Multistate Essay Examination subjects present.

Business Associations

In practice, much of the business-associations subject has to do with the choice, formation, structure, financing, and control of the organization. While advice on these topics is critical in a transactional practice, and these topics are certainly fair game for a bar-exam essay question, on the other hand these topics do not lend themselves readily to essay testing. The counsel that a lawyer would give as to the choice of organization form, for instance, would often depend on more variables than an examiner could readily insert into a fact pattern and would not in any case lend itself to the kind of binary, yes-no conclusions that objective or objectified tests require. Instead, the business-associations topics that bar examiners more-readily test will have to do with the powers, rights, duties, and liabilities of the various persons and entities having interests in or relationships with the business. Those persons or entities may include incorporators, officers, directors, shareholders, managers, partners, agents, and employees, together with the corporation itself or its parents, subsidiaries, predecessors, successors, or assigns. The duties of loyalty and care are common, readily tested issues, as are the rights of shareholders, derivative lawsuits, and the potential liabilities of (for instance) shareholders, officers and directors, partners, and successor organizations. Agency law, including particularly the power of an agent to bind the principal and the specific form of that agent's authority (whether express, implied, apparent, or inherent) is another example of a common business-association issue. Even though you may regard the subject as one more fit for practice than a bar exam, pay close attention to these readily testable issues. See your state bar exam's topic and subtopic outline for more detail.

Family Law

In practice, family law is an increasingly complex subject. Taxation issues, employee-benefits law, real-property law, domestic-violence laws, federal and state criminal kidnapping laws, federal and state statutes on child support and its enforcement, guidelines and formulas for determining child support and spousal support and credits for either, and other peculiar enactments can all affect rights in separation or divorce. Add to that complexity swiftly changing family structures involving unwed parents, single parents, joint or separate legal or physical custody, parenting time and supervision of parenting time, grandparent custody and visitation, same-sex parents, guardianships, adoptions, and foster care. Then add the complexity of insemination, implantation, confidentiality or rights of egg or sperm donors, rights and interests of surrogate mothers, and other maternity, paternity, and acknowledgment or proof issues. Fortunately, because of the uneven, narrow, and swiftly changing treatment of many of these issues, bar examiners are unlikely to test a good number of these issues that make family law an increasingly complex practice area. What you are instead more likely to see on a bar exam are the foundational issues of what constitutes a marriage, the rights and obligations of spouses including under premarital agreements, grounds and procedures for separation, divorce, or annulment, spousal support, division of property including treatment of retirement and other accounts and joint or separate debt, and, above all, child custody and support issues. Examinees often feel that family law is an area in which they can shine because of the familiarity and relatively less technical and complex nature of these topics. You are fine to have such confidence. Just be sure that you do indeed know the core topics in this area. See your state bar exam's topic and subtopic outline for more detail.

Trusts and Estates

The subject of trusts and estates is a classic for essay examination, one on which many examinees reasonably expect to do well. The transfer of property at death is a relatively familiar, accessible, and non-technical topic, disregarding for a moment the precise and unfamiliar nature of trusts-and-estates law. Bar examiners can readily create relatively complex fact patterns out of family relationships and various items of property and papers (which may or may not meet the requirements to be wills) left behind by a decedent. Examinees more easily engage with these questions because everyone, other than the actual participants, enjoys a good family fight, if you will excuse the sarcasm. Indeed, one of the perils of trusts-and-estates questions is that an examinee might get emotionally involved in the question and even draw unintentionally on the examinee's own family experience. Bar exams are the time to use your head, not your heart. While assembling the facts into an appropriate tension to

63

reveal the legal issues requires attention and concentration, the natural subject matter often makes those challenges smaller concerns. The larger challenge to these questions can be recalling important, indeed dispositive, details of the statutory and code schemes. The law of intestate succession has its necessary fine points addressing shares of spouses, children, and more-remote descendants. The requirements for executing a valid will are also precise, even if not particularly numerous or complex. Be sure you treat the subject with that necessary precision. Otherwise, will challenges are a usual strategic trigger for testing trust-and-estate topics that may include construing will terms, age and capacity requirements, and undue influence or mistake. Competing transfers outside of probate are another likely trigger, as may be survivorship issues, adopted children, and children born to unwed parents. The hard topics in this subject area, topics that examinees likely hope examiners avoid, have to do with the classification of interests including in particular future interests. May the examiners be kind on your examination. See your state bar exam's topic and subtopic outline for more detail.

Secured Transactions

Many law students regard secured transactions as a difficult subject. The subject is not one in which many persons, particularly younger persons who have not yet purchased a home or financed a business, have substantial experience. Secured transactions is not an accessible subject like torts, criminal law, or family law but instead a somewhat arcane subject primarily of interest to those involved in commerce and finance. Secured transactions also routinely involve not the simple binary alignments of contract or tort disputes but multiple parties, like seller, buyer, purchase-money financing entity, other lenders or creditors taking security interests, subsequent purchasers, and judicial lien creditors, each having distinct roles and interests. Despite this complexity (or perhaps because of it), secured transactions are enormously important to commerce, underlying most financing, providing protections to creditors, and facilitating loans to grow businesses and provide consumer credit. Vast sums of money may depend on a lawyer's careful attention to detail. Bankruptcy and collections are both specialty practice fields for which knowledge of secured transactions is a prerequisite, as it can be for real-estate practice, construction law, development work, business-startup practice, mergers and acquisitions, contract review, corporate counsel, and indeed nearly any transactional or corporate practice. Thus, more law students should be taking law school courses in secured transactions rather than waiting to learn this important and difficult subject during bar preparation. Secured transactions is a challenging subject to learn in a brief bar-review course. If that is the position in which you find yourself, then roll up your sleeves and get to it. Once in practice, you are likely to appreciate having done so. See your state bar exam's topic and subtopic outline for more detail.

7 Conditions

Conditions Matter

To perform optimally, you must be fully familiar with your state bar exam's conditions including its format. As to format, you are very likely already well familiar from law school with multiple-choice and essay questions. You are less likely to be familiar with the increasingly common performance test. Subsequent chapters address each of the three formats, *multiple choice*, *essay*, and *performance test*, and how to approach them for best results, in much greater detail. You may already be skilled in at least one or two of those test formats, but you should still ensure that your skills are at their very best. The strict form of the question, though, is only one important condition as to the bar exam's overall format. You should also know the time allowed for each section of the bar exam, the points allocated to each section and thus its relative weight, and then specifics of the conditions under which you must perform. Consider those issues in the following sections after a brief summary of the bar exam's general format.

Format

Because states vary in bar exam sections and the time allowed for those sections, you should determine your state's bar-exam makeup and times as soon as you choose a state bar and plan preparation. Consider the multistate formats as examples. The prior chapter identified the subjects of the Multistate Bar Examination and Multistate Essay Examination. As that chapter indicated, the Multistate Bar Examination is a 200-question multiple-choice examination scoring 190 of the 200 questions. The

Multistate Essay Examination is obviously an essay-format test. The National Conference of Bar Examiners, which drafts both of those tests, also offers the Multistate Performance Test comprised of practice materials from which the examinee must draft a legal document, for instance a motion, brief, or memorandum. About one third of state bars adopt for their bar examination all three of these National Conference of Bar Examiners tests. The National Conference of Bar Examiners calls this comprehensive three-part bar exam the *Uniform Bar Examination*. Your state may adopt only the Multistate Bar Examination (the multiple-choice format), both the Multistate Bar Examination and Multistate Essay examination, or all three parts of the Uniform Bar Examination. The Uniform Bar Examination tests the six essay questions of the Multistate Essay Examination and two performance tests of the Multistate Performance Test on the bar exam's Day One and the 200 multiple-choice questions of the Multistate Bar Examination on Day Two. States using other configurations of the Multistate Bar Examination, essay exam, and performance test may require a third day or part of a third day of testing. Passing scores on the Uniform Bar Examination are around two-thirds of the possible 400 points, with the specific number depending on the state.

Time

Time may be the single most-important condition with which you must deal effectively to pass the bar exam. Well before the exam, indeed when you are practicing answering multiple-choice and essay questions, you should know the amount of time that you have to answer each question. In two three-hour sessions, the Multistate Bar Examination gives you 1.8 minutes for each of its 200 multiple-choice questions, which means that you should have completed 33 to 34 questions every hour. Falling behind and rushing through final questions is not a sensible option. States vary widely in the time that they allow for essay questions, from as little as twenty minutes to as much as an hour, so again, you must learn from the bar examiner what that time is and then prepare to manage that time properly. Practice under these time constraints. Accustom yourself thoroughly to time constraints so that they no longer affect concentration. Habituation to exam conditions is an important practice to ensure maximal cognitive performance. As you navigate the exam's time pressure, remain fully in the moment. As soon as you finish one question, forget it, and move on to the next question. Ruminating over a prior answer while you attempt to answer the next question will not improve the prior answer but will instead delay you in completing the next answer. See the chapter below on multiple-choice and essay questions for more detail on how to manage time when answering those forms of questions.

Writing or Typing

One of the bigger decisions that examinees make when their state's bar exam gives them the option is whether to write or type. For very-fast typists, the decision to type is relatively easy, just as the decision *not* to type is easy for very-slow typists. One reliable way of confirming typing speed versus handwriting speed is simply to choose a familiar page of text and then both write and type that page as far as you can get within one minute. An average writer records somewhere around thirty words per minute. If you are not typing at that speed, and you are instead typing slower than you write, then write the exam. Typing speed, though, is not the only consideration. Your handwriting's legibility may also be an issue. Even though some bar examiners may go to some trouble to ensure that they can read what you wrote, the more trouble they must take to decipher illegible writing, the more risk the examinee faces of doing less well than they otherwise would have done. If your state segregates typists from hand-writers, then the noise of keyboards may be an issue for you, warranting earplugs. The reliability of your laptop computer and anxiety over its proper functioning may also be an issue for you. Investigate, plan, and be thoughtful in your choice of handwriting or typing.

Facility

The test-center facility in which you take the bar exam may have some influence on your performance. Take responsible steps to minimize any negative influence. If you have completed all of your practice exams in the same secluded location, then you should especially think about habituating yourself to exam performance in other locations. Professionals of all kinds, including singers, musicians, actors, and other performing artists, sports figures, or trial lawyers, very often make special effort to rehearse in their final-performance location. Some of the reasons for doing so are obvious such as to ensure adequate light to read scripts or notes, adequate sound to hear one's own voice among other sounds and noises, and so on. Getting a sneak peek at your testing environment also helps to avoid any unanticipated surprises from the surrounding context.

Transfer of Learning

Another reason for rehearsing performance in its final venue has to do with *transfer of learning*. Whether we realize it or not, as we perform we take subtle visual, auditory, and tactile clues from the environment. The feel of the keyboard, desk, and chair, the look of the walls around the room and the slant of light through the window, and the hum of the heat or air conditioning or chirping of birds outside the window, all provide reassuring stimuli that support and prompt recall and performance. Try to visit your test center a week or more in advance of the bar exam. If you are able to do so, then take your study materials, writing implements, or laptop computer if you are typing, and just spend a little time going through the bar exam's motions. If you are unable to visit your test center, then be sure to move your practice to one or more other locations in or out of your home so that your mind gradually transfers, internalizes, and diminishes environmental clues. Transfer of learning improves not only by matching the environmental cues but also by matching your own internal emotional and physiological cues. You want to practice under the same fast-paced conditions under which you will take the exam in order to improve your learning's transfer to test conditions. This transfer is why replicating time constraints is important, so that you *feel* the same pressure during learning and improve your recall during testing. Ultimately, you need to achieve high accuracy in practice despite feeling the fast pace and stress associated with such high stakes. Even if you are unable to practice in the testing center itself, you can still recreate the other aspects of testing conditions. However, don't become too preoccupied with these details. Although they are important, they are nowhere near as important as simply investing frequent practice and rehearse. As stated earlier in the book, don't put off studying simply because you are waiting for the perfect environment.

Policies

Ensure that you have received, reviewed, and made yourself familiar with all bar-exam security and other testing policies. You should receive your admission ticket a couple or few weeks in advance of the exam along with details on testing-day policies. If these materials show your seat assignment, then examine it closely for any anomalies (light, noise, ventilation, foot traffic, or other distraction) that you think might interfere with your performance. If you see any issues with your seating, then promptly contact the testing officials requesting more information, a seat change, or similar accommodation. Gather all items that admission requires or permits including things like photographic identification, pens or pencils, erasers, calculator, laptop computer, electrical cord or battery pack, tissues, gum or lozenges, and of course your admission ticket. Ensure that you store these items in an accepted receptacle such as a clear plastic bag. Know in advance every procedure for what you may do, such as use the restroom during the exam, and every detail of what you must *not* do, such as leave your seat for any other reason until the proctor collects your exam materials. Familiarity with all exam policies and conditions will ease your mind and reassure you just at the optimal moment when the exam actually begins.

8 Management

Management Matters

Actively manage your bar preparation. One might think that management should go without saying. Preparing for the bar exam is the first very important professional task that you will attempt and accomplish. Why shouldn't you actively manage your preparation? You should employ your best skills, very like the ones that you honed while succeeding in law school. Employing your best skills includes *deploying* those skills, meaning thinking and planning with honest and effortful deliberation over how you will best manage your bar preparation. You could leave employing your best skills to default, doing whatever bar-preparation activities come your way in whatever order others recommend or require. School-based and commercial bar-preparation programs attempt to relieve you in part of the obligation of managing your bar preparation. Some of those programs tell you everything they think you should do in precise order. Resist the temptation to rely on others to do all of your management for you. Instead, actively manage your bar preparation from Day One. You know a lot about your own strengths and weaknesses. Use that knowledge to individualize and control your bar preparation.

Control

Management accomplishes more than you think. Control is a big part of learning. The more that you perceive that you control conditions, the more effort and more-effective effort you generally put forth. Oddly, that advantage of perceived control holds true whether or not you actually control conditions. Simply thinking that you are influencing things, even when you are not, produces the mental, emotional, and physiological stimuli that improve your discipline and concentration, and thus likely your overall preparation and probable performance. Learned helplessness is a sad state. Perceived control is a happy state. We should want to get up every morning believing that we can make a difference. On many days, we cannot and will not make a difference, but still the daily attitude of believing that we can and will produces the kind of consistency, character, and discipline that improves preparation and performance. Take responsibility for your preparation, and take control.

Location

Choosing and arranging the location that you will study is a clear and practical example of how you can manage your bar preparation for best effect. Be intentional. You may have been able to study for law school courses just about anywhere, especially by your second and third years. For bar preparation, think again of your first term of law school and how intentional you had to be to find and use an appropriate study location to make the significant adjustments that law school required. Bar preparation takes special dedication and adjustments. Consider afresh whether studying at home, the local library, in an office, or at some other location makes the most sense. A special temporary arrangement such as borrowing a friend's cottage, cabin, or bungalow, or housesitting for a traveling homeowner, may provide a perfect combination of comfort and relative isolation from distracting routines. You may find that intermittent retreat to an isolated location works well in combination with the discipline of office-based study and comfort of home-based study. The point is to plan, assess, and adjust location.

Accommodations

The accommodations at your study location also matter. Your study-space criteria should include not only reducing distractions but also for internet access and appropriate furniture and other conditions. Furniture would include a desk-chair combination with electrical power for laptop computer and also soft, comfortable seating. Periodically moving from desk to soft seating and back again can reduce physical strain and increase study hours. Good lighting is important and good *natural* lighting better. Be conscious of lighting's secondary effects on mood and energy, such as with seasonal-affective disorder. Acquire study aids like a whiteboard and large paper on pad and easel or to tape to the wall. Collect stapler, tape, paper clips, post-it notes, and highlighters. Arrange these items in an orderly manner and visible and accessible location to give you an immediate sense of support and control. Make your study place appear and operate as a command center reflecting your commitment to success. You will draw surprising energy and assurance from doing so.

Time

Law school probably taught you a great deal about managing your time effectively. Bar-exam preparation will teach you even more. What you learn about time management will help you in law practice, which depends on effective management of time. Time is not quite as linear as you think. At least, it has multiple subscales to which you can attend to improve your management. You are already likely a master of two subscales, *persistence* and *organization*. Keep exercising those scales. Yet study shows that law students are not so good at the next scale, *present orientation*, which means to remain in the moment to do what is at hand. Pay attention to what you are doing, not what you are going to do next. You may also not be so good at *perceived control*, believing instead that tasks are beyond your capability within the time available when in fact you are able to accomplish them timely. Keep telling yourself that you can do it because you probably can. You may also need to improve your *goal setting*, meaning not just knowing the big thing that you need to do but also breaking that big thing down into manageable interim objectives. Plot and plan small tasks including making time estimates for each, and then go do them within the estimated time until they add up to your big goal. Make wise time allocations in to-do lists, and then keep those obligations. Learn to set and achieve immediate and short-term goals that lead to your bigger objective, which is full command of all bar subjects and skills.

Energy

Without meaning to be too dramatic about it, one can also say that bar-exam preparation requires at least some degree of managing your energy. You have worked hard before. You know from preparing for law school exams what intense studies are like. Yet you probably devoted your all to preparing for law school exams only for the last week or two before those exams, not for six, eight, or twelve weeks. Imagine cramming for final exams not for a week or two but for the whole term. And law school exams, while important for grades and standing, were not the difference between professional licensure and professional limbo. In those respects, preparing for the bar exam is very little like preparing for final exams. Unlike law school exams, you cannot blast into bar-exam preparation, run at full speed for a short duration, and call yourself prepared. If you try, then you will quickly have that uncomfortable sense of running on fumes. You must instead pace yourself. You should think of it as spreading your energy out over the whole time of preparation. What you accomplish on Day 32 of preparation is just as important as, and maybe more important than, what you accomplish on Days 1, 2, 3, and 4. Expend significant energy every day in your preparation, but also hold a little something back for the next day. Don't run on fumes. Keep filling the tank so that you can drive hard but not recklessly.

Pressure

One bar-preparation condition that you can and should manage is the pressure of the bar examination. Probably everyone who takes the bar at least momentarily considers the possibility of not passing it. Doing so is completely normal. You would be abnormal if you did not feel some pressure to avoid not passing. Indeed, the pressure of not passing can be a useful stimulus even if the reward of passing is a more-positive and thus more-fruitful stimulus. Yet some examinees dwell on not passing the bar more than others. While considering negative consequences can provide an appropriate even if limited stimulus, *dwelling* on negative consequences can produce anxiety. Of course, admit the high stakes, including the delay in licensure, financial cost, and employer and family explanations. But do not elaborate and extend the negatives into fear that feeds anxiety. Every negative has a corollary positive. To develop appropriate stability, even equanimity, dwell on the positives. Anticipate the inspiring swearing-in ceremony, the new job and increased income, and admiration of family members and friends. Let the positives give you peace and grace under pressure.

9 Skills

Skills Matter

The specific skills that the bar-exam requires matter to your success. Many examinees make learning or re-learning substantive law their primary bar-preparation goal. The bar exam does test substantive law — a lot of it. Learning or re-learning, organizing, and recalling substantive law remains important to your bar-exam success. Yet recalling law will in itself get you almost nowhere on the bar exam, just as recalling law would alone hardly do anything for a client. Essay examiners give little credit for outline dumping, that is, for simply stating quantities of law, even accurate law, when you do not connect that law to the facts, apply it in an articulate analysis, and use it to draw sound conclusions. Simply knowing lots of law may not help that much on multiple-choice questions, either. Instead, bar-exam skills largely involve application of law, just as law practice involves application. Nothing frustrates a client more than a lawyer who spouts lots of law without knowing what to do with it. Few things frustrate examiners more than an examinee who knows lots of law but who does not connect that law with the exam's problems. Bar-exam skills, like lawyer skills, involve organizing information, discerning relevant facts, identifying law issues, solving problems, and writing clearly, all while managing time. These skills require special forms of active study rather than passive study of substantive law.

IRAC

The primary reasoning skill that the bar exam requires you to exercise is the issue-rule-analysis-conclusion or *IRAC* skill that you learned in law school. That the bar tests a lawyer's fundamental reasoning skill should be no surprise. Lawyers use IRAC so much that examiners would surprise us if they tested only other forms of reasoning. Do not underestimate IRAC's power and prevalence for bar-exam success. Both multiple-choice questions from the Multistate Bar Exam and essay questions on state portions of exams require that you quickly identify the law issue. Examiners draft fact patterns to raise specific issues that specific rules resolve. They begin with the rule and its associated issue, crafting the fact pattern around the issue and rule. If you mistake a torts question for a civil-procedure question, or a criminal-procedure question for an evidence question, then you are very likely to recall and apply an inapplicable rule, reaching the wrong conclusion. Spotting law issues while recalling and applying the associated law rules is the fundamental bar-exam skill. Hone and use your IRAC skills. The chapter below on essay examinations addresses the IRAC construct in considerably more detail.

Diagnosis

Consultants who coach examinees on re-taking the bar exam frequently diagnose the failure to use IRAC as the primary re-take cause. Low-performing examinees tend to adopt a scattershot approach, which is really no approach at all. Examinees without issue-spotting skill quickly assume that a question is about one law subject or rule when instead the question's fact pattern raises a different issue invoking a different law subject or rule. Examinees without IRAC skill will often see the correct issue but jump to a conclusion without recalling and applying the rule. Or they will see the issue and know the rule but make no analysis, leaving their conclusion unexplained and incorrect. Or they will see the issue, know the rule, and apply the rule but reach no conclusion. The IRAC method imposes structure and logic, which is exactly what examiners want to see. The IRAC method is so powerful that it also serves as the reliable way to diagnose performance problems, whether on multiple-choice or essay questions. Did you have the right issue? Then did you have the correct rule? Then did you make a reasoned analysis? Then did you draw a sound conclusion?

Logic Model

Despite the demonstrated value of the IRAC method and the chorus of counsel in its support, some graduates just resist its use. If you count yourself among those unbelievers, then consider adopting an alternative logic model. One method begins with acknowledging the question (the equivalent of an abbreviated issue statement) and then using an *under, here, therefore* rubric. After the word *under*, state the law, rule, or procedure that you recognize governs the issue that the question implicates. After the word *here,* acknowledge the relevant facts while articulating how your law, rule, or procedure applies to them. For your *therefore,* draw the conclusion that your analysis compels. A similar alternative is to begin with your conclusion, what you feel preliminarily is the correct answer to the question, in a twist to IRAC known as CRAC (conclusion, rule, analysis, conclusion). After stating your preliminary conclusion, then state the law, rule, or procedure that compels that conclusion. Then explain why the law, rule, or procedure compels that conclusion. End by concluding once again, but more articulately or firmly than you did in your initial conclusion. The advantage of CRAC over IRAC is that you get right to the point. You answer the question right up front before even beginning your analysis. The disadvantage of CRAC is the same thing: you are answering before analyzing. If you adopt the CRAC method over IRAC, then practice qualifying your initial conclusion, and be more than willing to modify that conclusion if your analysis proves it wrong. The overall point remains that your answers must have some structure to them, or you will find yourself flailing around, confusing your scorer, and missing substantial points.

Learning

Learning the many rules necessary to prepare to write and reflect this kind of critical, structured judgment is of course your big bar-preparation challenge. You have been learning law throughout law school, and so you should already have substantial skill for re-learning law and learning more law during bar-exam preparation. Keep in mind the basics of what you are doing when learning law. You are not simply memorizing rule statements, although memory is an important aid. Sometimes rote memorization gets dismissed as unimportant. This unfair criticism throws the baby out with the bathwater. Your memorization of basic facts, terms, and laws is the foundation upon which your more-complex legal skills depend. However, you must go beyond the memorization and extend your knowledge to new and unfamiliar cases. You are placing rule statements into organized frameworks on which you can draw for the claims, charges, elements, factors, definitions, tests, or other conditions to evaluate whether certain factual premises satisfy those conditions. Learning, though, must include your ability to articulate those conditions as rule statements. You must be able not only to draw on the rules within their frameworks but also to state those rules in ways that show that you know how they operate. To ensure that you can apply the rules that you learn, you should be able to give examples and non-examples of every rule. That fundamental skill is in effect what lawyers do for their clients.

Protocols

We all use protocols or mental routines (the fancy word for which is *heuristics*) to reason through situations and make decisions quickly. As rule based and procedure oriented as law is, law practice especially is filled with protocols for everything from filing a motion to recording a deed and executing a will. Legal reasoning works in similar fashion. As you learn law, you are learning steps for analyzing whatever law issue or problem presents itself for resolution. You analyze the validity of a will in one manner, whether an injured person can prove a negligence claim in another manner, and whether Congress had the authority to regulate certain commerce in another manner. You may think that law's protocols involve many complex steps, but in fact protocols work best when they are no longer than three to five steps. Any longer protocol becomes too hard to remember. Instead, professionals who must learn and follow elaborate protocols break them down into memorable stages. Whether an injured person has a negligence claim begins with the four-step protocol of duty, breach, causation, and damages. If the same problem becomes how the person would prove breach, then the protocol involves considering whether the person has direct or circumstantial evidence, or can show violation of a safety statute or industry standard, or can rely on the doctrine of res ipsa loquitur. If the same problem presents a federal-law governmental-immunity defense, then the protocol becomes whether the defendant's actions were discretionary rather than ministerial, or involved another exception for active-duty military service, postal delivery, and so on. Recognize that as you learn law, you are developing hundreds of these small but highly powerful and useful routines.

Contrasts

An almost-equally powerful skill that you are exercising when learning, recalling, and applying law is to develop contrasts and distinctions among the concepts, principles, claims, charges, and other forms of rules. As you solidify your law knowledge and its proper use in application, you are gradually distinguishing one concept from another. A defendant violating a safety statute has a subtly different effect in supporting a plaintiff's negligence claim than does the defendant violating an industry standard. Many jurisdictions treat violating a safety statute as negligence per se or draw a presumption of negligence, while violating an industry standard typically permits only an inference of negligence. Indeed, to understand the distinction between violating a safety statute and violating an industry standard, you also need to distinguish negligence per se from a presumption or inference of negligence. As you prepare for the bar, investigate and accentuate these sorts of distinctions. You obviously must distinguish first-degree murder from second-degree murder or manslaughter. Yet look beyond the big distinctions among claims and charges to the subtle distinctions between the best-evidence and parol evidence rules, and between moving for judgment as a matter of law or new trial. The best way to tease out the subtle differences among concepts is to identify examples where the concept *almost* fits but does *not* fit because of minor differences. These close-but-not-close-enough examples will help you in defining conceptual boundaries and learning how concepts connect to each other. Every time you confirm your knowledge of one rule, contrast it to your knowledge of a related rule to the point that you are able to give contrasting examples of the application of each rule.

Reading

The bar exam tests a special kind of reading and comprehension. Although you must be a good reader to pass the bar exam, reading comprehension does not necessarily mean that you must love to read, be able to read massive amounts of material quickly, or have a delicate taste for the quality of written material. Indeed, some reading affinities such as enjoying a special turn of phrase or appreciating plot and character can actually distract you more so than aid you. Rather, the bar exam requires that you read efficiently with special concentration to recognize the law words such as *domicile, motion, tenancy, charge,* or *defense,* assemble the law-practice contexts whether involving pleading claims, considering contract clauses, or counseling clients, and identify the factual stimuli triggering the rules that you will apply to resolve questions and problems. The latter skill, identifying fact triggers, may be the most subtle of these reading skills. Fact triggers are often simple verbs reflecting actions such as *agreed, sold, regulated, transported, slipped,* or *fell.* Fact triggers also often depend on actors such as *officer, shopper, seller,* or *resident* and relative roles such as *lender* to *borrower, mechanic* to *owner,* or *landlord* to *tenant.* Fact triggers may also be adjectives such as *weak, careful,* or *skilled,* or adverbs such as *knowingly, negligently, voluntarily,* or *deliberately,* suggesting knowledge, skill, state of mind, or intention. Fact triggers also often include outcomes or results such as *injury, loss, gain, damage,* or *profit.* Read for any data that defines the actors, actions, intentions, and results because these circumstances establish the strategic contexts that trigger your law recall. While you read throughout law school in that fashion, you must sharpen those same reading skills for the bar exam. Your reading while preparing for the bar exam, and then your reading for the bar exam itself, must be especially active. You should stop reading and check yourself, the moment that you find that the words are simply passing before your eyes as you daydream about other things. For critical phrases that you must learn and recall, read aloud, even touching each word on the page as you say it, so that it gains your full attention and burns itself into your memory. Read as if every word counts. It probably does, particularly on the bar exam, and particularly for the Multistate Bar Examination's multiple-choice questions, which include few irrelevant words. Read with attention to any word that defines, alters, or distinguishes the fact pattern. As the next two sections show, the basic sequence is to read critically, think critically, and write logically.

Thinking

The greatest skill to reflect on the bar exam is the skill of *critical thinking*. You may justly feel that with so much law to know and so many questions to read and answer that your bar-exam performance will be more topical and hurried than deliberative and critical. Don't fall into the trap, though, of thinking that the bar exam is primarily a measure of cherry picking right from wrong answers. While the exam is long and comprehensive, you are not skimming lightly over the surface of subjects like skating on a frozen pond. Instead, dive in deeply wherever you find the opportunity to use your critical judgment. As comprehensive as the bar exam is, examiners still can and do test fine points of law within problems that require thoughtful consideration and analysis. Even on the 1.8 minutes that you have for each Multistate Bar Examination multiple-choice question, think and choose smartly, discerningly, thoughtfully. Especially on essay questions and performance tests, demonstrate that you are a sound, rational, logical, and insightful thinker who treats all of the data carefully and thoughtfully. Use your mind actively and every relevant bit of law knowledge that you have acquired. Wherever possible, show that you are a discerning and incisive lawyer, one whom your examiner would hire. Think smart, write smart, and *be* smart.

Writing

Writing is obviously an important bar-exam skill but in some respects in a way peculiar to the profession. You need have no particular skill for some of the writing skills that other professions and pursuits value. You need not be good at developing a theme or characters, holding your reader's attention with fresh images or usages, or using alliteration, rhyme, or dialogue. You certainly need not be literary. Instead, your writing must be workmanlike, precise, clear, and reasonably articulate, the more so, the better. You are not looking to win literary awards. Instead, your writing needs to be very practical and clearly present your points. Your grammar and punctuation must convey what you intend, and little more. Literary but less-conventional constructions like the frequent double dash or semi-colon between complete sentences are generally unnecessary adornments unless they are natural constructions that fit your flowing and highly readable writing style. Make sure that as you write, you assume the role that the examiner has given you. If the examiner assigns you the role of representing one side, then don't write as if you are advocating for the other side. If the examiner has made you the theoretical arbiter or clerk to the judge, then write from that balanced viewpoint rather than as an advocate for one side or the other side. If the examiner asks you for counsel to the client, then give counsel to the client. If the examiner makes you the advocate, then advocate, or if the mediator, then mediate. If you are to predict, then predict, or if to evaluate, then evaluate.

Law Terms

The practice may seem rudimentary at this point, but learn the meaning of every word that your bar-review materials present to you. Do not skip words that you don't understand. Stop, look up the word's definition, and rehearse that definition until you understand and recall it. Keep a log of those words that you learned to which to return to check your recall. Build glossaries of key words in each subject. Remember that key words and phrases are the building blocks of your more advanced skills. Even the fanciest of structures crumbles if its foundation is weak. Memorize definitions precisely, especially for key terms of art and law standards, using acronyms or mnemonics. A *mnemonic* takes the first letter of each word of a law definition, framework, or list of factors, conditions, or elements, as triggers for instant recall. For example, OCEAN is the examinee's best-known mnemonic, listing the five conditions *open, continuous, exclusive, adverse,* and *notorious,* for adverse possession. If mnemonics don't seem to work well for you, then try repetition and rehearsal aloud to trigger oral and aural recall, or visual figures, charts, and diagrams. Flashcards can be especially useful tools when used properly, meaning actively, in which you are forcing yourself to express memories before turning over cards. Memory remains a powerful tool for professionals even in this you-can-Google-that society. You need a strong conceptual framework before you can decide what you should be searching for on Google, which is why not everyone has instantly become a genius despite open access to sophisticated search engines. Develop a strong ear, eye, and pen for law phrases, especially those reflecting constitutional clauses and key code, statute, and rule phrases. Don't speak and write like a plumber, farrier, or farmer but like a judge and lawyer.

Precise, clear, and correct vocabulary is critical to strong exam performance. You must know the meaning of law words to answer multiple-choice questions correctly, and you must use law words correctly to score well on essay questions. Use bar preparation to continue to expand your vocabulary and learn to write with a lawyer's eye and ear for precise terms.

Errors

The above sections summarize the primary skills that you need to develop and exercise to pass the bar exam. Again, with general credit to the text *The Essential Rules for Bar Exam Success*, consider here the obverse of those skills, that is, those habits, attitudes, and practices that will lead you to *not* pass the bar exam:

- The biggest error has to do with *not preparing for the bar exam*. Examinees who don't prepare give several excuses, none of them sensible. Some say that they took the bar exam as just a practice exam. Please: practice using *practice* exams, not the *real* bar. The bar exam is not practice. Practice is practice. Others allow family, friends, or play to distract them. Whatever the excuse, throw it aside, and prepare for the exam. You won't develop the skills that you need without doing so;

- Another common error has to do with working too much and too long while attempting to prepare, so that the examinee is *preparing without time*. These examinees may be fully committed to preparing for and passing the bar exam, but work absorbs so much of their time and energy that they never quite put in the time and energy. It is easy to get caught up in day-to-day responsibilities such that your short-term commitments interfere with your long-term goals. Examinees who did especially well in law school, have a great law job in which they are already working, and are overconfident in their skills, should especially watch for this hazard;

- Another error has to do with *preparing without commitment*, as in just going through the motions. Some examinees explain that they are not sure that they *want* to practice law. The bar exam, though, determines whether you *may* practice law, not whether you *must*. Take the bar exam seriously whether you are sure about practice or not. Who really knows about liking practice until you start? You cannot start until you pass the

85

bar exam. Preparing without commitment and passion will not develop necessary skills;

- A related error has to do with *preparing passively* rather than actively. Some examinees are committed, want to pass the bar, and make the time to do so, but then fall into a habit of just watching or listening to the assigned recordings and doing the assigned readings without actively engaging the practice materials. They do not take responsibility for their active skill development, instead entrusting it to others as if they will acquire skills by osmosis rather than use. You must practice the skills actively. Passive participation is not preparation;

- A related error has to do with *preparing shallowly* rather than deeply engaging the subjects with intelligent thought. You are preparing to practice law in which the matters clients entrust to you are significant. Memorizing the bare minimum of subjects at such a topical level that you do not grasp how they work when applied including the objectives that they can achieve will not serve your future clients. You want to be an effective lawyer, not an ineffective one. Examiners can quickly recognize shallow reasoning. Prepare with real thought;

- Another error has to do with *preparing without strategy*, particularly strategies for answering multiple-choice and essay questions. The bar exam is a strategic challenge as much as it is a law-knowledge challenge. Just as you wouldn't try a case to a jury without first having some familiarity with courtroom procedures, so too, you wouldn't take the bar exam while unfamiliar with its question protocols and formats. You need to be a good test taker to pass the bar exam. Develop your strategic knowledge of how to answer questions quickly and correctly.

10 Practice

Practice Matters

By now, the message should be clear that to prepare successfully for the bar exam you must practice the actual performance that the bar exam requires. One almost wishes that you could simply sit down for the bar exam and start writing out and reproducing your best outlines. Unfortunately, the performance that the bar exam expects is not reproduction of outlines. And yet too many examinees prepare as if reproducing outlines is all that the bar exam entails. They write and re-write outlines, and read and re-read outlines, without taking the next step of applying the law that those outlines summarize. Outlining law and memorizing outlines is fine and even necessary as far as it goes. You need to know the law, and not just a little law but a lot of law. Yet that form of preparation does not go far enough. The bar exam requires *using* the law, not just recalling the law. You must practice the performance. At some point, and the earlier the better, you must get beyond your notes, summaries, and outlines. Some coaches recommend daily practice of multiple-choice and essay questions beginning as much as six months or even more before the exam. When preparing for the bar, concentrate on producing relevant *output*, particularly practice exams, more so than amassing hours of input, like watching or listening to recordings, reading materials, and going over outlines. In that sense, treat bar-exam preparation more like you would work than you would like traditional studying. The law firm that hires you will want your output, your performance on critical tasks, not simply your input, like logging hours in the law library.

Active Learning

Again, do not hold too long and too tightly to your notes and outlines without beginning to practice the performance. If you are doing so, then you may simply misunderstand how learning proceeds. More studies are showing that the earlier one makes an effort to solve a problem, the better one learns the criteria and procedures for resolution. Practicing problems before you have the knowledge base solidly down can improve the speed and reliability at which you acquire that knowledge base. Problems, whether essay or multiple-choice questions, or performance tests, help you create, correct, and confirm the logic constructs, schema, frameworks, and connections that aid recall. Some describe the difference as one between *passive learning*, meaning activities like reading, listening to audio tapes, and watching videos, and *active learning*, meaning practicing problems and otherwise engaging your skills in the learning. Frequent and active learning with feedback is your most important consideration for building the knowledge and skills you need to tackle the bar exam. Don't just create an outline once and then spend inordinate amounts of time staring at the outline. Practice problems. Practice more problems. Keep practicing again and again. When you finish a practice question, promptly review the answer and any explanation, even if you chose the correct answer or feel that you did well in writing a response. Rehearse the terms, concepts, and laws on flashcards. Rehearse them until you know them all. Then keep rehearsing until you know them quickly. Finally, keep rehearsing until your performance flows smoothly like water. You want to be both accurate and quick with your knowledge so that you don't hesitate when you are confronted with the bar exam. When you see law statements justifying an answer that you missed, read those law statements aloud, write them down, and rehearse them until you know the rule that led to the correct answer. Be as active in your methods and learning as you can be.

Timed Practice

You should practice under the same time constraints that your state's bar exam imposes. You may initially practice using more time than the bar exam allows, as you confirm your knowledge, develop your skill, and improve the speed and fluency of your reading, thinking, recall, analysis, and writing. Soon, though, you should be practicing using the same limited time as the bar exam allows. You need to learn to read, recall, reflect, reason, and express your answer at the speed that the bar exam's time requires and at the level that the bar exam's time allows. Discerning every nuance of a multiple-choice question by mulling it over for far longer than the bar exam allows, or writing masterful, highly articulate, beautifully constructed essay answers using two or three times the period that the bar exam allows, will not help you develop the speed and fluency that you need for the bar exam. A large part of the bar exam's challenge, and a large part of its value, has to do with your fast and fluent recall and use of law knowledge. Deliberate reflective thought is not an option. You must learn to read, think, answer, and write so readily as to make your performance nearly automatic. The only way to do so is to practice within time constraints.

Quantity

How much practice is enough practice is an open question that may well vary from examinee to examinee. Even while we all need and benefit from practice, some of us benefit from more practice than do others of us. Yet the sheer quantity of practice that some successful examinees have performed may surprise you and stimulate and challenge you to do more practice problems more regularly and effectively. For example, successful examinees report answering 20, 30, or 50 multiple-choice questions every day for weeks or even months. They may take periodic banks of 100 questions as the Multistate Bar Examination format requires. Bar-exam instructors may recommend completing at least 2,000 practice multiple-choice questions, while examinees have by scorecard counted taking over 5,000 practice multiple-choice questions. That large of a quantity may be unusual but may also help you adjust your own objectives and increase your practice. Successful examinees also report writing two to three essay answers every day while also reviewing those answers, accumulating into over 300 practice essay questions. You must answer a reasonably large quantity of essay questions in order to practice answers on all dozen subjects of the Multistate Essay Examination. Answering at least two to three questions each day would enable you to practice all dozen essay subjects with appreciable frequency.

Quality

The quality of your practice, though, matters just as much as *or more than* the quantity. When you are practicing multiple-choice and essays questions, you should also be studying your answers. Review the explanations for your correct answers to multiple-choice questions to ensure that you know *why* you got the answer right. Review even closer the explanations for your incorrect answers to multiple-choice questions to ensure that you correct your law knowledge and improve your application skills. Watch for patterns in incorrect answers. If you are missing questions especially in a certain subject area, then focus your studies in that area while assessing the quality of your subject-area resource and making appropriate adjustments. Your materials or outlines on that subject may be inadequate or incorrect. Look for other patterns in your essay answers when comparing and contrasting them to model answers. If you frequently miss issues, then you may need to take additional time to read essay questions and outline essay answers. If you frequently miss rules, then you may need more practice on writing rule statements quickly and fluently. If you frequently skip analysis, then you may need more structure to your essay answers to ensure that you are applying law to each issue. Spend time analyzing your performance even while practicing your performance. Make your practice *quality* practice, not just quantity practice.

Model Answers

Consider these few words about model answers. Bar examiners write model answers to each essay question. They do so to ensure the exam's integrity, guide scorers, assist examinees who do not pass consider an appeal, and assist examinees to prepare for the next exam or subsequent exams. In some states, examiners share questions and model answers with professors at the state's law schools for critique after the exam but before scoring answers. Those who help examinees prepare for the bar exam will also write practice essay questions and model answers. Do not let the model answers discourage you. Your practice answers and bar-exam answers will not look like the model answers. Model answers often include case names, case citations, statute quotations and citations, and other detail that enables anyone reviewing the model answer to discern the law sources.

Examiners do not expect you to memorize multiple case names, case citations, lengthy statute quotes, and statute citations. Your answer may be just half as long as the model answer, contain no case or statute citations, and yet score full points, provided that it meets the rubric that the examiner will draw from the model answer. Do not let the detail of model answers intimidate and depress you. Instead, learn to draw from model answers the expected rule, structure, and core logic of an astute examinee's timed answer, which will inevitably be without the detail of the research supporting the model answer. You are not, in other words, shooting to reproduce model answers. You are instead aiming to recall the memorable rule, write the sensible analysis, and reach the same sound conclusion as the model answer.

11 Essays

Essays Matter

Essay questions make up a considerable portion, up to half, of many bar exams. Your skill at answering essay questions matters a great deal to your bar-exam success. You will need to demonstrate several specific skills to pass the Multistate Essay Examination or equivalent essay-format questions drafted by your specific state. The National Conference of Bar Examiners states that those skills include each of the following:

- identifying the legal issues that the fact pattern raises, including separating relevant from irrelevant materials;
- showing that you understand the legal principles that resolve the issues; and
- writing a clear, concise, well-organized, and reasoned analysis of the legal issues.

Essay questions mimic a lawyer's core skills at issue-spotting, law recall, and reasoned analysis. Examiners are adept at using a single carefully chosen word or well-crafted phrase specifically to trigger your law recall and application. Note that these skills closely approximate the IRAC construct. While the call of the question will direct you to your task and may even identify one or more legal issues, you must still first identify the strategic interests and tension around those legal issues. You must then recall the law, showing that you understand it. And you must then apply the law in a reasoned analysis, reaching a sound and concise conclusion. Indeed, as you write your essay answer, use headings and phrases to signal clearly to the examiner that you are following IRAC format. Frequent paragraph breaks help the examiner recognize your IRAC structure, particularly when you begin paragraphs with topic sentences or even short phrases like *for the applicable law* introducing your rule section, *applying the law* or even simply *here* for your analysis section, and *in conclusion* for your conclusion. Consider next each section of a strong IRAC-format essay answer.

Issue

Because you will write your essay answer following the IRAC construct, first consider what identifying the *issue* entails. The call of the essay question may be specific enough that it not only describes your task but also identifies legal issues that you must resolve to complete the task. Even if the question already states the issue, then do not hesitate to place that issue in context when you start your answer. A well-constructed issue statement prepares the examiner to give you the benefit of every doubt while also guiding you in the rest of your answer. A well-constructed issue statement requires more, and does more, than simply state the law subject like "formation," "consideration," "hearsay," or "admissibility." An issue statement saying simply, "The issue is the confrontation clause," does not give the examiner any sense that you recognize the participant's competing interests and objectives. Rather, a helpful issue statement that guides you in crafting the rest of your answer while impressing the examiner with your skill is one that includes the action ("This question requires analyzing whether..."), parties ("... the prosecutor has grounds to charge the suspect..."), law ("... under the common law for homicides..."), and factual context ("...when the suspect admits having shot the decedent."). Notice the key words *whether*, framing the issue, *under* referring to the law, and *when*, referring to the facts. Use this *whether-under-when* rubric to construct your issue statement. Practice quickly writing complete issue statements that include the action, parties, law, and factual context like the following:

- "This case requires determining *whether* / the trial judge should grant the contractor's motion to dismiss the developer's case / *under* Rule 12 for failure to state a claim / *when* the developer's complaint omitted any allegation of duty."

- "The call of the question asks for analysis of *whether* the husband's evidence of the wife's affairs is admissible / *under* the Federal Rules of Evidence having to do with relevance and undue prejudice / *when* the parties' only dispute is over a division of marital property."
- "These facts present the question of *whether* / the trial judge should grant the debtor's motion for summary judgment of the creditor's claim / *under* Rule 56 for no genuine issue of material fact / *when* the creditor failed to present an affidavit or other evidentiary material in response to the motion."

General Questions

Some essay questions specify the issue, as the questions to which the issue statements immediately above would have done. Issue-specific questions may be how a trial judge should rule on a summary-judgment motion, whether a will is valid, whether an incorporator would be liable for a certain corporate obligation, or whether certain evidence would be admissible. Review past essay questions in your jurisdiction to discern whether they are issue-specific questions that you can answer in the above fashion beginning with a specific statement of the issue. Other examiners use general rather than specific questions such as to *evaluate the liability*, *address the duties*, or *discuss the rights* of certain actors, or to *evaluate the constitutionality* of a certain action or provision. While these general questions may appear to invite a broad and topical survey of possible issues, to the contrary model answers on past questions of this type will likely show instead that the examiner had one, two, or a small number of specific issues that the examiner expected you to spot and then address. These general questions are often *issue-spotting* questions as much as they are a test of your law recall and legal analysis. Bar exams are routinely tests of your law-recall and legal-analysis skills applied to specific fact patterns, not of your ability to list law topics without having analyzed their application. Again, review prior questions and model answers in your jurisdiction to confirm the examiners' expectations. You are very likely to find that even the general-seeming questions intend that you spot, address, and analyze limited specific issues. Focus your answer where the fact pattern and question clearly invite. Watch especially for words like *carelessly* or *deliberately*, and phrases like *with all due care* or *without any intent*, with which examiners intend to rule in or rule out those specific issues that the examiner expects you to address. Examiners routinely signal you *not* to address certain issues, just as they signal you *to* address certain issues. Forcing yourself to write an issue statement before you begin with your rule section and then your analysis section should help guide you to the significant issue or issues that the fact pattern triggers. Don't fall into the trap of skipping the step of stating the issue and then making broad law-topic surveys devoid of specific controlling rules that you can then analyze. You must recognize and state issues. Otherwise, the rest of your answer will suffer. Above all, be sure to do *exactly* as any question including a general question asks, such as to *analyze fully*, *discuss and evaluate*, or *identify and explain*.

Multiple Issues

Depending on the jurisdiction's testing practices, some essays may have multiple questions or a single question with multiple subparts. Obviously, you must answer each question and each subpart to receive a full score. Try answering the questions *in the order asked* even if you find the first question harder than others or would for some other reason prefer a different order. You may still get full credit for an out-of-order answer but may also annoy or distract the examiner whose model answer, scoring rubric, and expectation are that you will take the questions in order. Beyond that advice, consider that examinees tend to make two errors on essays with multiple questions or subparts: (1) answering fewer than all questions and subparts; or (2) giving a single answer that addresses all questions and subparts without distinguishing clearly what part of the answer addresses which question or subpart. The most-reliable way to ensure that you answer all questions and subparts in distinct sections of an answer is to *use headings*. If for example the questions and subparts involve disputing pairs, then your headings should so reflect as in *Buyer v Seller*, *Buyer v Seller's Spouse*, *Buyer v Mortgagee Bank*, etc. If by contrast the questions and subparts involve different legal claims between the same two parties, then your headings should so reflect as in *Defamation*, *Invasion of Privacy*, *Misrepresentation*, etc. As you read the questions and then circle back to read the essay's fact pattern, do not hesitate to note these headings as an outline for your emerging answer. Then, as you write the answer, be sure to confirm that you have addressed all noted headings. General questions to *identify and discuss all claims* or *evaluate all procedural options* will also often require an answer that addresses multiple issues. Once again, use headings to mark clearly what issues your answer addresses and to ensure that you are addressing all issues.

Rule

Next consider how you should address the *rule* statement that the IRAC framework requires. After giving the issue statement, you should next be stating the applicable law, meaning that which addresses the issue and will form the basis for your following analysis. When examinees follow their issue statement with a summary and discussion of the facts, examiners immediately suspect that the examinee does not recall the law. Essay questions are uniformly tests of law recall. An essay question may test one, two, three, or more law constructs, but the answer will always require knowing, recalling, *and writing* law. Do not skip the step of writing clear, concise, and confident rule statements, particularly those that will decide the issues. If you cannot immediately recall or are uncertain about the specifics of the law that the issue plainly implicates, then begin by writing what you do know and recall of that law. Writing what you recall often triggers what you know but have not yet recalled. A single-sentence rule statement ("Worker's compensation covers accidental injuries arising out of and in the course of work.") may barely suffice. Yet model answers will often elaborate the applicable rule into a good-sized paragraph that expands and expounds on that rule. Without simply dumping outline language that covers much more than the question requires, practice writing rule *paragraphs* of applicable law rather than a short sentence. State the rule, but then define terms or phrases within the rule. State the rule, but then state exceptions to or conditions for the rule. List elements or factors associated with the rule. If the rule has a three-part test, then write the three-part test. State the positive rule but then also its negative corollary ("Worker's compensation does not cover intentional injuries or injuries that do not arise out of or are not in the course of work."). Show the examiner not only that you can recall the rule but that you understand more of how the rule operates.

Rule Framework

Further strengthen your rule statement by placing it within its framework including the jurisdiction. A sound rule statement proceeds from the general to the specific. The statement's general part may include the jurisdiction. If you are writing an answer that depends on a peculiar state law distinct from other states' laws, then begin with a phrase like *under Michigan's form of no-fault law* or *as Indiana domestic-relations law treats child custody*. In doing so, you have first located the dispositive rule within the jurisdiction's broad scheme or code. Rather than then simply stating the one narrow rule, element, condition, factor, or definition that you have concluded determines the issue, show the examiner the law framework around that narrow rule. Introductory statements like *child custody is an equitable determination depending on multiple non-exclusive factors* or *products liability arises for manufacturers, distributors, and retailers in the business* can help locate the specific rule that you are about to address within its supporting framework. Absolutely, get to the fine point, but in doing so move from general to specific. Record the applicable rule concisely and precisely, apply it, show your analysis, and conclude. Yet by also reflecting the rule's larger framework, you ensure that the examiner appreciates how you arrived at that rule by distinguishing it from other bodies of law and selecting it from among other claims, elements, conditions, factors, or definitions. In a figurative sense, you put the rule in a box and tie a bow on it. You may also pick up points for addressing related rules that the examiner believes may have some bearing on the issue, even if you plan primarily to address the dispositive rule. Defenses may fall into this category, as may also remedies. Once you address what you are sure is the dispositive rule, discuss other arguably relevant rules, even if in the process you rule them out. The examiner may have ruled them *in*, meaning that you will have at least addressed them and in doing so probably gained some point or points.

Analysis

Probably the single most important but also most-overlooked skill in essay answers is the *analysis* portion of the IRAC construct that you will use in your essay answers. As you first state the rule, resist drawing in facts. Yet once you have articulated the applicable rule in a short paragraph that places the rule in its framework while expanding and expounding on the rule, then be certain in your analysis section that you draw in every relevant fact that the rule implicates. Application generally takes the form of *[conclusion] because [rule] when [fact]* or *[conclusion] when [fact] because [rule]*, as in these examples:

- The father should have custody *because* the established-custodial-environment factor easily favors him *when* he has had the children for the past three years;

- The landowner has no liability *when* the injured person had broken into the store *because* landowners owe no duty to trespassers who break and enter;

- The young woman is an accomplice *because* the evidence readily satisfies the specific-intent element *when* she helped plan the crime and *because* the evidence satisfied the furtherance element *when* she purposely drove her friend to the site of the crime.

The words *because* and *when* are your best friends in any analysis. Using the word *because* connects rule to fact. Using the word *when* draws facts into the analysis of the rule and its elements and definitions. If you are not using the words *because* and *when* frequently in your analysis, then you may simply be concluding rather than applying law and analyzing fact. Keep in mind that examiners are giving you the facts in order to make exactly that kind of close analysis. Examiners use extremely precise words like *diligently* or *intentionally*, and phrases like *with notice* or *without knowledge*, specifically to support and guide your analysis. Each word of the fact pattern is a signpost pointing you in one direction or another that the examiners expect your analysis to acknowledge expressly. If you fail to acknowledge those signposts, mentioning them in your answer and pointing out why they are significant, then you will lose those points that the examiner intended you to garner. Too many examinees simply state law and then state conclusions without drawing relevant facts into a well-developed analysis section. Your answer must include facts, not in simple summaries but in articulate analyses that treat the facts as satisfying or not satisfying the rule and its elements, factors, conditions, or definition. If your answer is devoid of facts, then you have failed to analyze and instead have probably only concluded. Do *not* make up facts, but do draw reasonable and appropriate inferences from facts while stating that you are doing so ("Subject to investigation, the facts suggest that the hunter was likely aware that the gun was loaded."). Work with the facts within the structure of the law, taking each element or important condition in order while making it clear to the examiner that you are doing so ("As to the first element," "Regarding the last element," "Now considering the rule's exception").

Conclusion

Too many examinees fail to conclude at all, or they at least fail to conclude articulately. You may well feel at the end of your thoughtful analysis that the conclusion, meaning the specific and firm resolution of the issue, is obvious. The conclusion is not obvious. No matter how articulate and even compelling your analysis may have been, the examiner will not conclude for you. Rather, the examiner expects to see *you* state the conclusion. Even if you have stated one or more subsidiary conclusions within or at the end of your analysis, make a paragraph break, write "In conclusion," and then write or rewrite a comprehensive conclusion that clearly resolves the issues. Essay questions on bar exams may be clearer in the conclusions that they expect you to draw than were law school essay questions. Law school was a lot about seeing both sides, finding the fighting issue that could go either way, or arguing policy and nuance. While some bar-exam essay questions may present close calls, and you should recognize arguments on the other side when they exist, examiners draft most bar-exam essay questions to have a correct conclusion. While an otherwise quality answer may gain substantial points even if you reach the wrong conclusion, you generally will not get full points unless you conclude clearly, concisely, and soundly. Answer the question. Resolve the issue. Avoid conclusions that say merely that an outcome *may* occur, as if the outcome was merely *possible*. Many things are possible, but examiners dislike it just as much as clients, judges, and law professors dislike it when you don't answer their question.

Judgment

That said, in practicing writing conclusions, you should find that you are adding subtle evaluations, conditions, or emphases that your analysis did not necessarily reflect but that mark you as a sensitive practitioner. Clients do not so much pay you to reason as to exercise judgment. Your analysis may well have sounded mechanical given that you had to address definitions, elements, conditions, or factors in logical constructs. You may have been uncomfortable in writing the analysis because it sounded more one-sided and less sensitive and nuanced than it should have. You probably omitted any reference to the law's policy or the seeming justice of the situation. To remedy the mechanical quality of a logical answer, and to show sensitivity and nuance in your conclusion without making the conclusion seem weak or mushy, consider using qualifiers like *definitely, very probably,* or *likely,* that indicate the probable outcome while suggesting some thought of the contrary. You can also balance your firm conclusion with qualifying considerations that show your ability to foresee a contrary outcome. Consider the following examples:

- "In conclusion, the trial judge should definitely dismiss the developer's case under Rule 12 for failure to state a claim, where the developer failed to allege a duty, although the trial judge should permit the developer to attempt to amend unless amendment would be futile."
- "In sum, the husband's evidence of the wife's affairs is likely admissible on the property-division issue as probative of fault in bringing about the divorce, although the trial judge must not give the evidence undue weight and may disregard it if satisfied that the parties shared fault in the marriage's demise."

Outlining

Strong essay-writing skills require more than IRAC organization. You should also consider in advance the extent to which you plan to outline an essay answer before beginning to write or type the answer. Whether you outline answers before writing them will depend to some extent on the time that your state's bar exam allows for each essay answer. Some states allow up to an hour for each essay answer, while other states allow just twenty minutes per essay. If you have an hour to answer an essay, then taking ten minutes to read the question with care plus five more minutes to outline your answer before taking the final forty-five minutes to write your answer would make sense. If on the other hand you have only twenty minutes to answer, then reading for ten minutes and outlining for five minutes would leave you only five minutes to write the answer. Better instead to severely reduce outlining. Even with bar exams that allow for minimal reflection time, though, you should still be thinking about the structure of your answer as you read the question, spot issues, and formulate answers. A well-structured answer can *save* you time rather than *cost* you time. A few abbreviated notes like "Issue 1 AB v CD injury 2014" and "Issue 2 CD v AB trespass 2015" may keep your analysis on track and prevent you from forgetting issues that you must address. Even if you simply list (in one or two words) each issue as you read the question, then you will have a created a checklist against which to compare your finished answer.

Time

The bar exam makes time of the essence. Every minute counts. Again, this time pressure is why becoming fast and fluent during timed practice sessions is a critical part of your preparation. On exam day, your challenge begins with ensuring that you answer each essay question within the allotted time. Long before the exam, you should have determined the number of essays and allotted time for each session so that you can calculate and practice the same time per essay. For example, you may have three hours within which to answer nine essay questions, meaning twenty minutes per question. If so, then answer each question within twenty minutes without falling behind. While some examinees quickly review all questions in order to deal first with ones as to which they have more confidence, the better approach is to take the questions in their order. Taking questions out of order or skipping questions creates a risk that you will not answer all questions. Allocating time to different parts of your essay answer can also be a key activity to ensure that you address the fighting issues for which the examiner designed the question. As you read the question while listing the issues it raises, make quick time estimates (writing *2, 5, 10*, etc.) for each issue. You will thus have a roadmap for where to spend your time, dispatching easy issues quickly while saving your time to address at length the close issues.

Latent Awareness

Examiners cannot count what you don't put on the page. Examiners do not generally want outline dumping. Simply spouting a lot of irrelevant law does not generally earn you extra points. On the other hand, examinees frequently think one thing while writing another. More to the point, examinees often leave out the subsidiary thoughts that led them to the analysis and conclusion that they wrote or typed on the examination. Low essay scores are often the result of failing to record that subsidiary thinking, recording instead only its end result. *But that's what I meant*, the low-scoring examinee will often argue when challenged by the question's model answer spelling out the rationale. What you *meant* makes no difference to the examiner. What you *wrote or typed* makes the difference. Force yourself to record the subsidiary latent awareness that has guided you to the sound conclusion. Bar examiners will reward that guiding rationale. We call it *legal analysis*. Write or type what you are thinking when reaching sound conclusions, not just the sound conclusion itself. Write what you are thinking, spelling things out as plainly as time permits. You get no credit for any thought that does not reach the page.

Roles

When answering essay questions, be sure that you have placed yourself in the role that the call of the question requires. The call of the question may have placed you in the role of trial judge, appellate judge, judicial clerk, or lawyer advocate for one side or the other. Knowing your role, and addressing it in your answer, may be critical to your answer's score. If your answer assumes that you are the prosecutor when you are instead defense counsel, then you may completely miss the question's point. Even if the call of the question does not expressly assign you a role, consider the differences that roles may make to your answer. Qualifying your reasoning with phrases like *the plaintiff may argue* and *the defense will likely maintain* or even *a reasonable juror might conclude* demonstrates to the examiner that you think strategically like lawyers think. Indeed, whether or not the question assigns you a role, hone your strategic sense by initially assuming a prosecutor's role when reading a criminal-law question but a defense lawyer's role when reading a criminal-procedure question. Similarly, take the plaintiff's role when determining whether a fact pattern gives rise to a tort claim but the defendant's role when determining whether the same pattern gives rise to a defense.

Writing

Bar examiners do not expect your highest-quality writing. They know that you are writing under time pressure. Examine answers that received high scores on past exams, and you will see that the vocabulary and sentence constructions can be basic, and the grammar, spelling, and punctuation can include mistakes. Relax, or at least don't beat yourself up over your inability to produce perfect writing under considerable time constraints. Especially do not expect to produce highly articulate creative writing. That said, though, the quality of your writing can subtly influence the scorer. Indeed, when your writing is so rough as not to convey your meaning, then the scorer will not be able to give you the points that you expected to earn. If you feel that you have an extra minute or two to devote to an essay answer that you have completed, and you cannot think of ways to improve your answer's substance, then consider correcting some of the more-significant grammar, spelling, or punctuation errors, and otherwise improve the clarity of your writing with headings and paragraph breaks, topic and summary sentences, and transitions. Make your answer easier to read and understand if you can do so with minimal time. Use shorter paragraphs and sentences rather than longer ones. Remember that your scorer will be reading many answers and will benefit from every paragraph break, transition word, and declarative plain-English sentence that you can muster in the time allotted. Think Hemingway, not Faulkner.

Tone

Consider a note, too, about the tone with which you write. Your readers are bar examiners, which depending on the jurisdiction means practicing lawyers, sitting judges, law professors, or other professionals intimately familiar with the law who write and evaluate bar-exam questions. Because the examiners who read your essay answers will also be reading dozens or hundreds of other answers, trust that you cannot possibly bore them. Indeed, practice *stating the obvious*. The examiner may have already read the obvious implication in dozens of other high-scoring answers, but the examiner still needs to read it in *your* answer. In a sense, make your effort to bore them with yet another complete and correct answer. You need not write to catch their attention, not like you might write to catch the attention of a busy judge, client, opposing counsel, or insurance claim representative. Your writing need not and indeed should not look distinct from other sound and articulate writing that addresses the issues, rule, analysis, and conclusion in the manner for which the examiner designed the question. While you should always write thoughtfully and articulately, your tone need not be overly formal or stuffy. You may write in a conversational tone as you would in a memorandum to a law partner whom you respect and trust. On the other hand, avoid humor, catchy phrases, colloquialisms (particularly those that may be unfamiliar to some readers), and other eccentricities, all of which are likely to distract the examiner from routine scoring and thus be more likely to hurt than help.

Errors

Consider and avoid these common errors in essay answers. State a rule in its logical order, major premise before minor premise, rather than *reversing the rule's order* beginning with the small point before making the big point. State applicable law as complete rules, rather than simply using *buzz words* repeating law phrases without communicating the sense of the rule. State the rule before stating the exception rather than *stating exceptions without the rule*. If the rule that you are identifying and applying is a federal rather than state rule, or a minority rule or rule distinct to the jurisdiction, then say so rather than *assuming that the examiner knows the difference*. Examiners recognize when examinees use buzz words as if *name dropping* to sound knowledgeable but actually disguising shallow law knowledge. Use proper law vocabulary and terms rather than *inarticulate substitutes*. Define key law terms rather than *omitting important definition*. Use reasonably short and declarative law statements rather than *joining unrelated concepts* in compound or complex sentences just to make your writing *sound important*. Choose and argue relevant rather than *irrelevant facts*. Although most of the facts in an essay question may be relevant to some issue, be sure to connect relevant facts to the right rather than wrong issue. Join facts to rules in thoughtful analysis rather than *repeating facts aimlessly*, devoid of connected rules and reasoned analysis. Do not *simply list facts* without connecting each fact to its associated rule in a reasoned analysis. Identify the rule or element that facts address rather than *discussing facts while hiding the law those facts address*. Make your law-fact connections logical rather than using *illogical non-sequiturs*. State the results or outcomes of your analyses rather than *assuming that the examiner sees* the result or outcome. Avoid each of these errors, and adopt the proper practice instead, and you will have substantially increased your probability of bar-exam success.

12 Multiple Choice

Multiple Choice Matters

Your performance on the Multistate Bar Examination's multiple-choice questions is as important an ingredient to your success as any other thing that you can do to pass the bar exam. You have no way around it: you must do reasonably well on the bar exam's multiple-choice questions. You may feel, as many examinees do, that you are better at essays or perhaps will be better at a performance test if your bar exam has one. You may believe that as a strong writer, you will do well enough on the essay section of the test to bring up your multiple-choice score to an overall passing level. You may even feel that you have just *never been good* at multiple-choice questions, as if being good at multiple-choice questions is an attribute with which one is born or not born. If these statements sound like you, then put aside all such thinking now. You can and will improve your multiple-choice skills and scores with appropriate resources and concerted, believing, and discerning effort. Multiple-choice questions require certain skills that you can and must learn, hone, and practice. Make your goal to do well enough on multiple-choice questions not to have to have your other work carry you through. Commit to making multiple-choice questions your strong suit, not weak suit.

Design

As any law graduate knows perfectly well, multiple-choice questions begin with a fact pattern that examiners call the *root* or *stimulus*. Questions then provide enough procedural context to support the call of the question that examiners call the *stem*.

Questions in the Multistate Bar Examination style then offer four answer choices that examiners call the *options*. Yet the National Conference of Bar Examiners gives other helpful clues to how examiners design Multistate Bar Examination questions. First, examiners design questions so that you should be able to answer *without reading the options*. Of course, you should read *every* option because you must choose the best one. One option should supply you with a definitively correct answer. But depending on how effective your bar preparation has been, you should nonetheless have a good sense of what the correct answer is even before reading the options. That design means that you should be reading the options primarily to *confirm* an answer you have already discerned. Answer options do not, for instance, supply additional facts for you to process to choose the best answer. This benefit of developing an answer before finding one among the options is another reason why it was important to practice your flashcards by stating answers aloud before turning the card for the answer. You want to force yourself into confirming a choice before looking at the possibilities. Second, examiners design questions to test only one rule. Answer options may present several alternative rationales, each reflecting a different rule, but the fact pattern and question should require knowledge of only the one rule that the correct answer reflects. Third, fact patterns have the minimum number of actors necessary to support the question. You won't find extra figures whose roles and actions have no bearing on the question. Fourth, fact patterns use roles (baker, plumber, employer, etc.) rather than proper nouns (Bill, Mary, Gerry, etc.). You shouldn't be confusing actors and actions. Trust that the National Conference of Bar Examiners drafts sound and fair questions.

Signals and Triggers

Because of the large number of questions and thus necessarily small number of facts in each question, and that the examiners are testing subtle rules, every word of the facts can be consequential. Even more so than in the case of essay questions, examiners use words and short phrases as signposts and signals. Certain words like *contractor* and *subcontractor* or *lender* and *borrower* will construct and highlight the parties' relationship. Watch for words that define the critical relationship. Other words usually having some law content, like *owner*, *title*, *claim*, or *charge*, must trigger your recognition of the tested law issue. Watch for words that highlight the law issue. Other words, often adverbs like *carefully* or *unintentionally*, or prepositional phrases like *without knowledge*, must rule out other possible issues so that you focus only on the tested issue. Don't miss these rule-out markers. In its few remaining words, the fact pattern must also give you the data, such as dates or perhaps clues to an actor's state of mind, to answer the question. Recognize that relevant data. Practicing many multiple-choice questions, where you promptly review answers and explanations, has the effect of honing your skill at recognizing and relying on signals, signposts, and triggers.

Question Call

For strong multiple-choice performance, you must pay particular attention to the call of the question or *stem*. Obviously, if you read and construe the question call incorrectly, then you are very likely to choose the wrong option. The calls of Multistate Bar Examination questions are usually sound in their construction. The committees drafting and approving the questions, and the psychometric expert guiding the drafters, generally eschew the too-easy-to-confuse negative question calls such as, "Which of the four defendants would *not* be liable?" or "Which of the following outcomes is *least* likely?" If you see a negative question call, be especially careful to follow it closely rather than mistakenly read its negative request in the positive. The question calls can, though, have awkwardly formal, cautious constructions, as in "Which of the following would be the most likely basis for the court's ruling granting the motion?" or "On what rationale would the court most likely award judgment against the homeowner?" Read awkward question calls in their more-direct meaning, such as, "Why grant the motion?" or "Why would the homeowner lose?" When necessary or helpful, quickly translate the question call into something firmer and more obvious to guide your selection of the one right option. When you see questions that include phrases like "the most likely basis," "most likely rule," or "most likely award," the examiners are acknowledging that more than one option may be plausible, which will not generally aid in your analysis because you are still looking for the one correct answer. Simply ask *why*, expecting that one answer will be clearly correct even if other answers appear possible or even plausible.

Make your best effort to recall the rule that clearly justifies the one correct option.

Options

One of the distinct features that examinees observe in multiple-choice answer options is that they often pair a conclusion such as *yes* or *no*, or *granted* or *denied*, with a justification. Often, the justification begins with *because* before reciting a law, rule, or principle, as in *yes because summary judgment is appropriate in the absence of a genuine issue of material fact* paired with other options like *no because summary judgment is inappropriate when the evidence raises a genuine issue of material fact.* Indeed, two options are often *yes because* or *granted because* while the other two options are *no because* or *denied because.* The construct of two options beginning with the same conclusion *yes, yes,* and then *no, no,* or *granted, granted,* and then *denied, denied,* require you to both reach the correct conclusion and also know the justifying rationale or dispositive rule. It is often not enough, in other words, to reach the correct conclusion without also knowing the supporting law, rule, or rationale. In many questions, examiners balance the conclusions equally in pairs of two as just shown, in which case the examinee must know the rationale (or be able to rule out a false rationale) no matter which conclusion the examinee draws. In other questions, examiners supply three options each of which draws one conclusion, but with different rationales, and only one option with the opposite conclusion. Do not prefer either conclusion simply because one conclusion has more or fewer options among which to choose. In other words, a single *no* option may be correct even if the other three options are all *yes.* Strategies of that type mislead. Use your law knowledge, not game strategy.

Qualifiers

As just indicated, *because* is a common unconditional qualifier to distinguish among options that draw the same conclusion. *Because* is not the only qualifier. Examiners also use *if, unless, provided that* or *as long as,* and other conditional qualifiers when the fact pattern has a latent ambiguity. Conditional qualifiers test your logic skills, the kind of skills that should be fully familiar to you insofar as they enabled you to get a qualifying LSAT score to get into law school. Most obviously, the law, rule, principle, or statement following the unconditional qualifier *because* implies a straightforward logical justification connecting the fact pattern to the conclusion, as in *this option answers the question because the following rule logically compels that answer.* Examiners may occasionally substitute the modifiers *since* and *as* for *because*, each meaning the same thing that the rationale compels the conclusion. By contrast, conditional qualifiers *if, unless,* and *provided* serve a slightly different function. The law, rule, or principle that follows a conditional qualifier like *if* may clarify which law the undisclosed and imaginary jurisdiction follows, for instance a majority or minority rule. Multistate questions can often involve non-uniform law in which the examinee may know the law subject but have legitimate question over which of two or more rules apply in the imaginary jurisdiction. Conditional qualifiers like *if, unless,* and *provided* will often confirm for the examinee that the question expects the examinee to apply a specific rule among several possible options as in the following examples:

- *Yes, if following the traditional premises-liability classifications.*
- *No, provided that the modern foreseeability test applies.*
- *Granted, unless in a contributory-negligence jurisdiction.*
- *Denied, as long as the rules permit pleading amendment.*

Conditional qualifiers like *if, unless,* and *provided,* can also clarify or confirm different reasonable interpretations of the facts. The short fact patterns of a multiple-choice question cannot possibly resolve every possible interpretation into one. The fact pattern may leave you leaning toward one interpretation but uncertain that you have inferred as the examiners expected. The justification following conditional qualifiers can confirm that you are drawing the intended inference, as in the following examples:

- *Yes, if the man's status is that of a trespasser.*
- *No, provided that the explosion was reasonably foreseeable.*
- *Granted, unless the owner's actions constituted consent.*
- *Denied, as long as the conspiracy evidence is plausible.*

Distractors

Another feature of Multistate Bar Examination questions is that all three incorrect answers will be credibly attractive options. Conventional wisdom suggests that one or two options will be obvious throwaways, while the other options will present deliberately close calls as to which answer is the best option. Conventional wisdom is wrong. The National Conference of Bar Examiners intends that the correct answer be clearly correct and clearly the best answer but also that *all three remaining options* be credible distractors. You certainly won't find any humorously wrong options intended to entertain you along the way. Credible distractors are often correct but irrelevant statements of law that simply do not apply to resolve the call of the question and support that answer option. Distractors can also be incorrect but plausible-sounding rule statements including such things as a minority rule where a majority rule applies, a rule where an exception to the rule applies, or an exception where the rule applies. Distractors can also be incomplete statements that do not go far enough to resolve the question. Distractors can also misrepresent or misconstrue the facts that the fact pattern just gave you. They can also deliberately but subtly swap roles, for instance perpetrator for victim, movant for non-movant, or proponent of the proffered evidence for opponent of the evidence. Because all three incorrect options will be credible distractors, you should make more effort to answer the question as you read it *before reading the options*. Reading the options before you make any effort to discern the answer may mislead you to seize upon and incorrectly rationalize an attractive distractor. Also, because all four options will be credible, and the three wrong options credibly attractive distractors, you should train yourself to read all four options even when you are confident that you know and have located the correct answer. You may instead have chosen an attractively credible distractor.

Procedural Context

Question design, though, is not quite as simple as facts (root), question call (stem), and answers (options). After or in the midst of the fact pattern, questions must also supply the procedural or practice context, meaning the judge-lawyer-client-opposing party part that creates the strategic tension. Examiners deliberately vary the procedural and practice contexts for the calls of the questions. Each call of the question is not as simple as a straightforward evaluation like "Does plaintiff have a claim?" or "Do the parties have a contract?" Rather, examiners include many different procedural and practice contexts involving client intake and interview, factual investigation, pleading, discovery, pretrial motions, alternative dispute resolution, trial events, post-judgment proceedings, appeals, office practice, meetings, and transactions. Getting the context right is its own skill, requiring special concentration. You may know the law and understand the facts but misread and misunderstand your particular procedural stance or practice role. Don't rush through the procedural and practice context. Here are a few of many possible examples:

- "How should the trial judge rule on the objection?"
- "Which would be the best method of discovery?"
- "Would an appeal be available to the employer?"
- "What is the effect of the officer's testimony?"
- "Which is the best advice regarding the claim?"
- "How would the creditor best enforce the judgment?"

Approach

While the approach may seem unnatural and forced, practice reading the call of the question first before going back and reading the full question. You may also find it helpful to scan the answer options quickly before reading the fact pattern. The examiner designs the fact pattern of a multiple-choice question to trigger your law recall. Read any fact pattern, and you should notice legal issues that spur law recall. When you read the call of the question first, you learn the procedural context and, along with it, confirm the law subject area, especially if you also scan the answer options and those options confirm the subject area. When you then return to the top to read the full facts, those facts should be triggering relevant rather than irrelevant law recall. By reading the call of the question first and scanning the options so that you already know the law subject, the facts will trigger relevant law, while you ignore false triggers of irrelevant law. Put simply, you can read a criminal-procedure fact pattern more quickly and confidently knowing in advance that it is a criminal-procedure question than you would if you mistakenly guessed that it was a fact pattern and question having to do with evidence, property law, or some other subject area. Once you have quickly read the call of the question and maybe scanned the options to get a sense of the law subject, and then read the full fact pattern carefully, recognizing the issue and recalling and applying the law as you do so, you should be able to answer the call of the question without even looking at the options. Allow and indeed encourage yourself to do so. Preserve and amplify in the back of your mind, rather than squelch and silence, those tenuous hypotheses that your mind generates as you read the fact pattern. Then formulate an answer as you finish reading the call of the question and before reading the options. The best option should then jump out at you, free of the attractive but incorrect distractors. Also, read and answer every multiple-choice question in order. Unlike some multiple-choice exams, with the Multistate Bar Examination *you face no penalty for wrong answers.* Thus, *answer every question, even if you must guess.* Some examinees adopt a practice of skipping hard questions, expecting to return to them after completing the rest of the exam. Skipping questions introduces the stress and hazards of not having time to return, losing track of which questions the examinee did not answer, and starting to answer questions out of order so that the examinee records multiple wrong, unintended answers. Rather than skip a hard question, choose the best answer but mark the question to return to it later if you have the time. While you may mark as many as a dozen or even two dozen questions, many examinees finish with thirty minutes or more of extra time, giving them time to return to every one of those marked questions.

IRAC

Here we go again: the IRAC method of reasoning is not only for essay questions but has its own application to multiple-choice questions. The above sections of this chapter should already have shown you how important the skills of spotting the issue, recalling and applying the law, and concluding are to answering multiple-choice questions. Multiple-choice questions are not some peculiar matching game divorced from legal reasoning. They are instead routine and highly structured tests of exactly what lawyers do day to day in analyzing law questions. Recognizing that you are using IRAC skills to answer multiple-choice questions can go a long way toward reinforcing the same skills that you will need for both essay and multiple-choice questions. Moreover, IRAC analysis is the primary way in which you can diagnose and improve your multiple-choice performance. When you miss a multiple-choice question, take yourself back through your thoughts on that question, asking first whether you spotted the issue, then recalled the rule, then applied the rule correctly, and finally drew the correct conclusion. Use the answer explanation in conjunction with the IRAC method to discern whether you are missing answers because you fail to spot the issue, fail to recall the rule, fail to apply the rule, or draw illogical conclusions. Using IRAC to diagnose your performance issues can help you strengthen the weaker aspects of your performance. You may need to practice issue spotting, or learn more law, or sharpen your analytic skill, or simply be more logical about your conclusions. IRAC is king here as elsewhere.

Wrong Options

Obviously, you will not immediately know the answer to every question. Many questions will involve choosing between two or three options that each appear plausible. In those situations where two answers both look correct, your challenge is not so much to choose the correct option as to reject the *incorrect* option. Multistate Bar Examination success has much to do with rejecting subtly incorrect options in favor of choosing wholly correct options. Indeed, even when you know that you have identified the correct option, you should confirm that the other options are incorrect. To identify an incorrect option, first recognize that to be a correct answer an option must be *entirely correct*, not just correct in part. Usually, in these close-call questions, you are not looking for an option that is *entirely* incorrect but only *partly* incorrect. So how are Multistate Bar Examination options incorrect? Some options misrepresent the facts just given. When the facts in the question's root say one thing and an option says anything different about the facts, rule out that option. An option cannot correctly contradict the facts. Nor can a correct option over-extend the facts or decide a fact issue that the root leaves open. Examiners deliberately write incorrect options that go too far with the facts including in resolving factual disputes. Next, rule out options that state incorrect law. Examiners will write incorrect options using outdated law, overruled law, law overstating or understating actual requirements, and simply nonsensical statements that sound like law. Then, rule out options the conclusion of which or rationale for which sounds incorrect. Options are sometimes wrong because they have the correct conclusion along with a correct rule but the rule does not compel the conclusion. These options present non-sequiturs, often attempting to use, say, a tort rule to justify a contract conclusion. The rule is right but the application wrong. The option's rule must match the rule that decides the issue. Don't choose a negligence-concept option when the fact pattern and question call raise an intentional-tort issue. Match option rule to fact-pattern rule. Options are also sometimes wrong because their rationale is overbroad, especially when they include absolutes like *never* and *always*. Options are also sometimes wrong because another option is somewhat more clear and precise in the way that the rationale compels the conclusion. Choose the more-precise option over the one that leaves ambiguity.

Time

As indicated in a chapter above, the Multistate Bar Examination requires that you answer 200 questions total in two three-hour sessions of 100 questions each, working out to 1.8 minutes per question or 33 to 34 questions every hour. One relatively simple and accurate way of keeping track of time is to figure that you must complete a little more than one question every two minutes. At 30 minutes in, you should have completed about 17 questions, while at one hour in, you should have completed about 34 questions. Halfway through at the hour-and-a-half mark, you should have completed 50 questions. Two hours in, you should have completed about 67 questions, and two-and-a-half hours in, 84 questions, to complete 100 questions by the end of the third hour. The sequence for every half hour is thus 17, 34, 50, 67, 84, and 100 questions. You cannot answer all questions at once. Looking ahead to answering 100 questions in a full three hours may unnerve you. Don't look ahead. Answer one question at a time while periodically checking your progress. With effective bar-exam preparation, you should find yourself quickly ahead of time, enough so that you can pace yourself. If you can build a small cushion of time, say, getting five minutes ahead early, then that cushion can relieve time pressure, which should make you even more efficient at reading, reflecting, and answering. Do *not* stick on questions. Remember that ten questions are throwaway questions that the National Conference of Bar Examiners will not even count against your score. Otherwise, every question has equal weight. If you just don't know the answer to one question, then mark whatever answer seems best and move promptly on because the next question and each question after it will have just as much value. Keep moving. Don't let tough questions sap your confidence. Let easy questions boost your confidence.

Finishing Early

Following the above approaches, and with effective study and substantial practice, you may well finish the two three-hour Multistate Bar Examination multiple-choice sessions with ten or twenty minutes or more to spare. If in your practice sessions you find yourself finishing way too early, then slow down your approach. Finishing ahead of time can nonetheless provide good benefit in that you have time to go back to check and confirm or change answers. Don't hesitate to do so. Make good use of extra time to confirm or correct answers. You may recall the frustration of getting an answer correct the first time but changing it to a wrong answer when re-reading the question and second-guessing your analysis. Yet research on whether sticking with the original answer or switching to another answer shows that examinees typically *benefit* from changing answers. The reason that second-guessing can seem hazardous is that examinees find it hard to forget the times when changing answers led to a wrong answer. We remember our losses and regrets much more than our successes. You do want to avoid reading too much into a question because examiners do expect you to figure out the answer from a single reading. However, if upon review a different answer seems like the better choice, then odds favor that changing to the new choice will improve your score. If you finish early, then by all means, reread your answers and change wrong answers.

Errors

Examinee errors on multiple-choice questions fall into familiar patterns. Some examinees fail to construct the fact scenario as the examiner wrote it. Sometimes this error is the result of the examinee knowing too much about similar fact patterns, for instance from having worked in that non-law field or having had a similar event happen. If the fact pattern seems familiar to you, then don't let your experience mislead you to add facts that are not present or change facts that are present. Go with what the facts tell you, not with what you think would or should have happened. Other examinees fail to construct the procedural and practice context, and construe the call of the question, as the examiner wrote it. For instance they may frequently swap roles, mistakenly assuming that the *employer* filed the motion when instead the *employee* filed the motion, or misreading *sustain* to mean *overrule* in the context of an evidentiary offer. Read procedural and practice context, and the question call, very carefully. Other examinees just don't know the law well enough to avoid attractive correct-but-inapplicable law distractors. Be sure to bring your full substantive law knowledge to bear on multiple-choice questions. Law practice is for lawyers who know law. Learn the details, not simply the broad concepts. Other examinees fail to reason logically and analytically. They do not spot the issue, recall the rule, and apply law to facts to rule elements and conditions satisfied or not satisfied. Don't forget your analytic skill on multiple-choice questions. Work carefully through multiple-choice questions as you would essay questions. Diagnose your pattern for missing answers, and correct common mistakes that you discover in your practice answers.

Guessing

When you don't know the law and thus do not know the answer, no simple strategy like always choosing option C, or always choosing the longest option, shortest option, or only option deciding the question the other way, will save you. The National Conference of Bar Examiners uses psychometric experts to ensure that examinees cannot game the Multistate Bar Examination. Yet even when you do not know the one single correct option, you may know just enough to influence positively your probability of choosing more rather than fewer correct options. Out of a 200-question exam, you are likely to be unsure of a good number of answers, enough answers that making better choices on uncertain answers will improve your score, even if only slightly. Slight improvement may be all that you need to pass the bar exam. If you must guess because you cannot recall the applicable law and no answer clearly appears to be the correct answer, then choose an option strategically. Your strongest strategy then is to rule out incorrect options in the manner that a paragraph above describes. Do not grow too frustrated at only being able to narrow the number of attractive options. Narrowing your guess to just two options substantially increases your chance of a correct answer. Increased probabilities matter. Use every bit of your knowledge, even when and indeed especially when your knowledge is incomplete. Your knowledge will also be incomplete at times in practice. Following reasoned hunches can be a helpful exam strategy, even if in practice you would instead do the research. When all else fails, and you have nothing to distinguish two or more options, then avoid options that simply repeat results without supporting logic or rationale, such as a conclusion that a homeowner should prevail because he owns the home, or a contractor should prevail because he had a contract. The Multistate Bar Examination tests applying law to facts. Choose options that do so. Then move on to the next question with a fresh attitude. Whether the prior question was hard or easy has nothing to do with how you should answer the next question. Every new question is a new opportunity for success or error.

13 Performance Tests

Performance Matters

Many state bar exams include not only the multiple-choice questions of the Multistate Bar Examination and essay questions either from the Multistate Essay Examination or of state design but also the National Conference of Bar Examiners' Multistate Performance Test. The first reaction of an examinee who learns that the examinee's particular bar exam has a performance component is often to groan because a performance test means one more set of conditions to learn and skills to master. The second reaction of an examinee to a performance test, though, is often to celebrate because performance tests give the examinee everything that the examinee needs to perform, relieving the obligation to learn, memorize, and recall additional law. The Multistate Performance Test does not assess law knowledge but rather lawyer skill. Indeed, the Multistate Performance Test deliberately presents a fictitious jurisdiction so that you must rely on the law that the question presents. The Multistate Performance Test involves two 90-minute sessions each involving one problem that requires the examinee to draft a document that lawyers commonly produce in practice. While 90 minutes may sound like a lot of time, it is not. You will likely find that you must perform with similar speed and fluency that other parts of the bar exam require. Some states adopt only one of the two 90-minute sessions, while other states adopt both 90-minute sessions. The National Conference of Bar Examiners' Uniform Bar Examination employs all of the Multistate Bar Examination, Multistate Essay Examination, and Multistate Performance Test.

Components

For each of its 90-minute problems, the Multistate Performance Test supplies examinees with a *file* of source documents. Those source documents supply all of the relevant facts and many irrelevant facts, just as source documents do in practice. One of those source documents is the supervising lawyer's brief memorandum telling the examinee what the examinee is to draft, whether a motion, brief, client correspondence, contract, settlement proposal, discovery plan, closing argument, will, or some other lawyer work product. The other source documents may be notes, statements, transcripts, pleadings, correspondence, medical records, police reports, news articles, and other materials typical of law practice. Each performance question also supplies a *library* with the statutes, case law, or other law sources necessary for the examinee to produce the work product but also including irrelevant source materials. The examinee then draws the relevant facts from the file and law from the library to produce the requested document, simulating law practice.

Skills

The Multistate Performance Test or other state performance tests thus require examinees to exercise several practice skills that multiple-choice and essay tests may not require at all or may only require within the much narrower performances of choosing an answer option or writing an analysis. The National Conference of Bar Examiners states that the Multistate Performance Test requires sorting relevant facts from irrelevant facts, analyzing legal-research materials, applying law to fact so as to resolve the client's issue, addressing ethical issues, communicating in writing, and finishing within the allotted time. Performance tests generally require a much more-challenging and rigorous separating of relevant from irrelevant facts and construct of the fact pattern. Examiners may also deliberately create fact contradictions, requiring the examinee either to resolve the contradictions where the materials allow, or to indicate in their work product the way in which a lawyer would investigate the contradiction. The performances require legal analysis and law application typical of an essay question but often expressed differently in the work-product form, such as a motion, contract, discovery plan, or will.

Performance tests thus stress effective written communication skills. On the other hand, performance tests give the examinee the controlling law, merely requiring the examinee to locate it within the code, cases, or other limited library materials, again a different skill than the straight-up memory work of law recall.

Approach

Performance tests, like multiple-choice and essay tests, require practice to optimize chances for success. If your state's bar exam has a performance test, then give it the attention that it is due. Your doctrinal studies in law school and bar preparation for the multiple-choice and essay portions of the exam will likely make you familiar with the law subject area of the performance test. Yet you cannot and need not study law to perform well on this test because the examiners give you the law in the performance test's library. Instead, the performance test requires that you prepare for the test conditions and performance itself, not that you study more law. Performance-test materials are sufficiently voluminous that you should plan a substantial portion of the 90-minute session, as much as a third or half of it, for active file review and library research. Begin by reading the supervising lawyer's short memorandum, near the end of which you will learn what you are to do (the form of work product). Then search the file for any law-firm instructions or protocols for what you are to produce. The test may even supply you with an example work product. Now you know more about what you need to produce. Then read the library for the law, starting with cases first, reading oldest to newest, and then statutes. Older cases give you the law framework including explaining the statute. Newer cases give you special rules, definitions, and exceptions. Statutes give you controlling detail. Then read the full file with an eye for the detail that you need to do what the memorandum said to do.

Time

While you should immediately discern the called-for work product so that you can focus your review and research, and you may using the above approach pretty quickly determine the first steps for what you need to produce, you should not be drafting the called-for work product in the first few minutes of the performance test. You may be outlining promptly but not drafting. If you begin drafting too soon, then you will probably be deleting much of your work and wasting that time. Examiners deliberately make the fact patterns sufficiently complex, and the legal research sufficiently precise, to test your ability to survey, synthesize, and think. Stream-of-consciousness prose, outline dumping, and mental purges are not for the performance test. Rather, the test requires that you think and communicate strategically, exactly that for which you should hope. You went to law school to practice, not to answer multiple-choice and essay exams. A good general guide is to take up to fifteen minutes to read and review the memorandum, instructions, protocol, and any example document, fifteen minutes to read the library materials, and fifteen minutes to read the file materials, noting and outlining along the way. You need to be drafting though by at least halfway through to give you a full forty-five minutes for drafting. Gain every minute that you can in your reading and review so that you have more time for drafting.

Organization

The greater challenge of a performance test is to identify, prioritize, and organize the information, both the facts and law, in the short time allowed for answer. While in law practice you might have an afternoon or even a couple of days to review a file and perform research on a matter while musing its issues as you handle other matters, the 90 minutes of a performance test require a highly intentional approach to organization. You don't have the time to review, re-review, and search deliberately for that particular data, whether a name, date, location, statutory clause, or case-law detail, that you discovered on first reading. One tactic to locate and organize relevant data quickly is to use the cover pages to the file and library to note that key data. The file and library should each include a list or table of contents on their covers. Those lists or tables give you a ready-made place for recording key information. You can certainly circle the key information on each page and write brief margin notes, although re-locating those pages may remain a problem. Folding the corners of pages having key information so that the point of the folded corner points directly at the key information is another technique that can quickly call your attention to information that you feel your work product must address. Be sure though that you are gathering the information necessary to do as the examiner has requested. Produce the assigned work product meeting the client's objective, not something else.

Communication

One of the peculiar features of a performance test is that the examiner may direct the work product for which it calls to any number of different audiences, each having a different level of law-and-fact knowledge and different expectations as to communication style and tone. For example, if the question calls for client correspondence, then your focus may be on plain-language articulation of the legal issues, without formal citations, and with an approachable but confident and authoritative tone. A question calling for a brief would require your work product to have more legal language, less explanation of basic law terms, more citations, and greater argumentation but with a highly respectful tone. A settlement demand might require greater description of the facts and evidence supporting them, straightforward law statements with appropriate citation, number detail, and greater advocacy. A contract might be more technical, clear, and precise, while bereft of argumentation or advocacy, and cool rather than warm in tone. The point is to vary your communication style or tone to fit the project's audience. Examiners specify the work product expecting you to adjust. You don't write to a client the same way that you write to a judge. Make sure, though, that your writing is clear and concise. Use shorter paragraphs and sentences than you would in practice. You won't have the time to craft complex paragraphs and sentences in a sufficiently readable form.

14 Behavior

Behavior Matters

So far, everything that you have read above may have been familiar to you or at least expected. The text above uses the vocabulary and constructs of lawyers and other professionals, familiar to any law student or graduate. Here, though, take a few moments to confirm the wisdom of some of the plans, programs, and practices advocated above, through the different perspective of behavioral science. Succeeding in law school is behavior. Studying for the bar exam is behavior. Practicing law is behavior. Your ability to successfully manage your own behavior underlies all of your personal and professional goals, so it would be helpful to understand how to use behavioral science to bring out the best in your performance. Social scientists have studied learning extensively and in the process have established certain principles and debunked certain myths. A lot of lore surrounds the subject of preparing for the bar exam. Some of that lore is unhelpful, inaccurate, and misleading. Some of it will frustrate rather than promote your bar-exam preparation. Use the following thoughts on behavioral theory and evidence for learning to evaluate the bar-preparation advice that you hear while putting a check on the myths that you may start telling yourself as your bar-exam preparation proceeds.

Motivation

You should understand your motivation and how motivation works. Sometimes we talk about motivation as if it is some inner quality. Behavioral science has shown that motivation can be any factor that pushes us towards goal-directed behavior. Motivation's sources include external factors, not just inner reservoirs of strength. The advantage to attending to those external sources of motivation is that you can do a lot to change external factors around you and therefore increase your motivation. Preparing for the bar is intellectually arduous, even if it does not entail the kind of physical effort, personal discomfort, and safety risk that other career-preparation programs entail. Bar preparation's steep intellectual challenge makes critical your motivation, impetus, effort, and constant inclination to prepare. You succeed largely because of the quantity and quality of your effort, not because you discover the kingdom's magic keys. It takes extended effort with no easy shortcut. But there are things that you can do help yourself in your commitment to that effort. Given that motivation toward effective effort is an important success key, you should be aware of both your strongest motivators and strongest distractors. The most obvious source of motivation has to do (if you will excuse a moment's gross overstatement just to make the point) with the eternal riches, meaning, and glory that come with passing the bar. Given how desirable and salient that reward appears to be, it would seem like that alone should be sufficient to inspire you towards progress. The truth is that passing the bar is not a powerful enough source of motivation by itself, as shown by the fact that many people do not make adequate progress in preparing for the bar examination despite their intentions. They strongly desire the outcome and feel that inner motivation should be enough to propel them towards success. It often does not. Big future rewards are not very effective in motivating you on a daily basis.

Feelings

Part of the problem is that your idle assessment of your progress, meaning how you *feel* that you are doing moment to moment and hour to hour, is highly unreliable, indeed often the opposite of your actual progress. Often, the better you feel moment to moment, the less learning-boundary effort you may be putting forward. Students in any program sometimes forget this lesson, thinking that education itself should be inherently rewarding. It is not. The *outcome* of being a competent professional is incredibly rewarding, but the *process* of becoming competent is difficult and even punishing in the short term.

When you invest time into preparing for the bar examination, the typical short-term outcome is an unpleasant experience. Preparing for the bar examination is hard work, maybe the hardest work you'll ever do. After an hour of study, it is easy to feel exhausted, while your only immediate reward for such hassles is a small improvement in your skills. Those small improvements can add up into making you a successful professional, but those who study for the bar often find it hard to feel that way in the moment.

Immediacy

Our natural inclination is to avoid hard work that has only small immediate reward, even if that hard work would lead to large delayed reward. You need to work against your natural inclination because those small-but-cumulative gains are important in the long run. You need to contrive rewards and conditions to push yourself past a difficult but worthwhile obstacle. Passing the bar exam might seem like your strongest motivation, but in truth the best motivators are those that you can arrange for frequent achievement. You can create daily sources of motivation by collecting data on yourself so that you can see the overall improvement in your skills. You can find frequent sources of motivation by enlisting others to provide you with social consequences for daily achievements or shortcomings. Daily sources of motivation require planning and doing something that doesn't come naturally. Look for external sources of motivation that you can regularly arrange for yourself. Don't blindly rely on some inner wellspring of motivation to carry you forward.

Procrastination

The Schedule chapter of the book addressed the time-management threat of failing to properly predict how much time one needs to accomplish goals. However, we must still deal with another time-management threat in the form of procrastination. Putting off until tomorrow what you can *and should* do today is your primary enemy in bar preparation, just as procrastination will be your enemy in your future law practice and is generally in life. A single big test at the end of studies on which your entire study result depends is a poor design for motivation and excellent design for procrastination. Put simply, the bar exam invites procrastination, when procrastination you cannot at all afford. This condition is part of the reason why the bar exam may feel like a large and scary threat. Rationally, it shouldn't be threatening. It is simply something that tests your collected skillset, one that you could readily acquire by practicing those skills daily. Just distribute your practice and study over time, and you'll do fine. The problem is that we are not inherently rational creatures. We often do quite poorly with small consequences that are only important when they accumulate, especially if that accumulation occurs over an extended period of time. Most of us could easily cite some self-improvement goal we failed to reach that required frequent effort for a minimal daily improvement. Physical fitness, weight loss, and similar goals are good examples of goals that require small cumulative gains. Unfortunately, study skills fall firmly within the category of small-but-cumulative gains. Bar preparation provides no immediate large benefit. Therefore, examinees often wait until they feel the pressure of an impending deadline before they start studying and then work frantically to get out from under the pressure.

Structure

Much of your education offset this natural tendency because your teachers often provided the consequences for you. If you didn't study, then you would fail a test or be embarrassed in class in the very near future. Bar preparation lacks this structure, so you need to artificially build in deadlines and consequences for yourself. The effective way to counteract the powerful single-terminal-test procrastination effect is to create and employ multiple staged tests leading up to the final test. Your challenge is in taking these staged tests seriously. If you continue to think that only the bar exam counts, then you may not put your maximum effort into the staged practice exams or may not take them at all. Bargaining with yourself, saying something like "it isn't a big deal if I quit early today and put in extra time tomorrow," is all too easy. You can too easily convince yourself that you still have time to make up the difference. You may, in other words, succumb to procrastination under the influence of the single-terminal-test effect. You must guard against this effect. Set up multiple deadlines and sub-goals in advance. If you can, then enlist the help of someone who won't tolerate you putting off your progress until tomorrow. Just as many people hire fitness coaches to help them manage the small-but-cumulative gains associated with physical health, consider a time-management coach to help you manage the small-but-cumulative gains of your bar-exam preparation. Find someone who will constantly push you to meet, not delay, your sub-goals and cheer on your interim successes. If such a person is not available, then you have to function as that person for yourself. *Do not bargain with yourself.* Putting that small amount of study time until tomorrow *will* hurt.

Cramming

Research consistently shows that distributed practice leads to better learning than cramming during mass practice sessions. Trying to cram for an exam also creates a high level of anxiety that can interfere with learning. Delaying your study may result in you discovering that you do not have enough time to adequately prepare. What you want to produce is what behavioral scientists call the *repeated scallop effect* in which you put forward maximum effort multiple times leading up to the terminal test. This effort will only happen if you structure multiple deadlines with enforced consequences for both success and failure. What will you gain if you meet a sub-goal? What will you lose if you fail to meet a sub-goal? If the answer is "nothing" to either question, then your self-management plan is too likely to fail. Remember that these sub-goals need to happen frequently. If the only consequences are "pass the exam" or "not pass the exam," then you may have a recipe for a procrastination disaster. Do not wait that long to experience the consequences if you want to motivate yourself *today.* Each interim practice exam should spur you on in repeated focused and intense studies, the cumulative effect of which is high performance on the bar exam as your final test. Beat the procrastination effect with multiple full-effort practice exams.

Distraction

A range of attractive activities set themselves against that core motivator of improving your practice-exam scores. Most examinees will have just graduated from law school, meaning that they have a new liberty, lease on life, and freedom. You may have delayed various gratifications throughout law school. Strong temptations can exist to pursue those gratifications at least in part before preparing for the bar exam and even while preparing for the bar exam. Family members and friends may expect you to lighten up on your former law school seriousness and partake in the joys of your new liberty. Rest, recreation, relationships, travel, pastimes, and acquisitions all beckon. You may have begun new work right after graduation at your new law firm or increased your work hours at the firm at which you were clerking during law school. Your deeper, full-time, compensated involvement in your law-firm work can be another powerful distractor from your core motivator of improving your practice-exam scores. One reason that these competing activities are such a strong source of distraction is that they often have a seize-the-moment quality to them. Social gatherings and entertainment opportunities may require you to participate right now or not at all. Bar preparation can always be delayed another day, or at least it seems that way. Your family and friends might even argue with you by pointing out that you can simply study tomorrow, so you should spend time with them today. The problem is how easily and quickly those delays accumulate until it is too late to study in a reasonable manner.

Deferral

Recognize how these distractors are competing with your core motivator. Do not dismiss their power or effect. Instead, acknowledge their competition both to yourself and to others. Then deliberately set them aside to the full extent necessary to *improve your practice-exam scores*. Recognize openly and frequently that you are only delaying, not forgoing, those opportunities. Let others know why you are temporarily sacrificing your social activities. Ask others to help with your self-discipline rather than compete with it. Make your sub-goals and progress publicly known so that others can be understanding and supportive. They may even become additional sources of support and motivation, rather than distractions, if you carefully explain your plan and rationale to them. Other opportunities for rest, recreation, relationships, travel, pastimes, and acquisitions, not to mention full-time compensated law-firm work, will all be there for you *after* the bar exam just as much and indeed more so than *before* the exam. Rest assured, too, that you will enjoy those pursuits much more after the exam than before the exam. You have no need to forego other gratifications entirely. Simply delay and defer other gratification until you can most enjoy it after having accomplished successful bar-exam preparation.

Other Variables

Other less-influential variables lie just outside of that critical tension between your practice-exam scores and their highly attractive distractors. You might find some motivation in the intellectual stimulation of bar preparation, just as you may well have found fascinating certain courses in law school. The problem with grounding bar-preparation motivation in the subject matter itself is the quantity of bar-preparation study. Your intrinsic interest is easily satisfied with just a moderate amount of exposure. Enjoyment is hard when you feel like you are drowning in the subjects rather than sipping at them lightly. Quantity makes *work* an unpleasant word, even for full-time employment in one's dream job. Instructor and peer approval can be significant motivators in well-constructed seminars, as can approval from family and friends when displaying knowledge in social settings. Yet those after-the-fact motivators won't work, either, for intense bar preparation. You need motivation for the process of studying now, not motivation to show off your skills later. The immediate usefulness of new skills can motivate learners, but the intense effort that bar-exam preparation requires leaves no time to use your new skills, from which unauthorized practice would in any case restrict you until licensure. The point is that none of these other variables are powerful enough to ensure reliable motivation. Although such future outcomes related to passing the bar may have been the impetus that started you on this professional journey, those delayed outcomes are weak sources of motivation for your needs today. Rather, your daily sub-goals and practice-exam scores, and their immediate consequences, are more closely tied to passing the bar. Those smaller but more immediate outcomes are the key to reliably motivating you and unlocking your future dream job.

Monitoring

Another advantage of frequent full-effort practice exams tied to ultimate bar-exam performance is that they aid you in time and task monitoring. At the outset, learners generally underestimate the time that specific learning tasks require. We just tend to think that learning will be easier than it is. So for example, an instructor assigns a reading, suggests or requires certain associated study activities, and announces a test to follow. Initially, the student will leave too little time for the reading and activities, and either come to the test unprepared suffering the resulting low score or have to scramble and cram to complete the assignment and gain the better score. Either way the student will have learned the time and effort, and possibly discerned other practices, that adequate preparation requires. Frequent interim practice exams enable you to hone your time and task monitoring. By taking data on yourself, you will discover how much you actually need to invest for success. Regular monitoring has another benefit in addition to more-accurate predictions of necessary time commitments. Watching improvements in your own performance over time can be very motivating. Create a visual graph of your improvements over time. Mark the average number of terms per minute you got correct on Monday, or use some other performance measure. Repeat this monitoring on Tuesday. Continue throughout the week, and then look at the direction of your overall performance. Small gains are often unrewarding without context. When you can see how each small gain steadily contributes to a larger overall improvement, those small gains start to become more meaningful. Watching your own data inch closer and closer to your goals can be exciting. Behavior that gets measured tends to matter the most to us. Frequent feedback is a source of both assessment and motivation. If instead you wait for the bar exam, without frequent practice exams, then you may well find yourself either unprepared or cramming. You will only have a single piece of feedback in the form of a final passing or failing score on the bar exam itself. This motivation will not be enough to help you accomplish your sub-goals but will instead lead to procrastination. Cramming at the end of a deadline is a very poor practice and ineffective strategy for such a comprehensive exam as the bar.

Myths

What are the myths affecting bar-exam preparation? One myth prevalent among learners even in graduate and professional education is that quality instruction and resources are sufficient inputs to motivate and produce adequate performance. The thought is that if you just sign up for the right bar-review course, find the right set of outlines, or work with the right study partner, then you will prepare adequately for the bar exam. What makes that thought an inaccurate myth is that the bar exam and preparation for it are simply too intense for attractive inputs to motivate adequately. Effective performance is too subtle for those inputs to work without rigorous assessment. You need frequent practice exams and frequent consequences along the way. A second myth is that scores on practice exams don't matter because bar takers can ramp it up under the pressure of the real exam. To the contrary, the bar exam may have just as many distractors as or more distractors than practice exams. If you do not perform well enough on practice exams to reflect bar passage on the actual exam, then you face a considerably more-difficult challenge. A final myth is that how effectively you concentrate when attending lectures, watching videos, listening to audio recordings, and reading bar-review materials, determines the quality of your bar preparation. To the contrary, you do not know the quality of your preparation *until you measure it*. You measure your preparation by performing the ultimate task, which is responding to bar-exam questions. Don't accept the myths. Go with the behavioral science and facts.

15 Results

Results Matter

Goes without saying, doesn't it?! You should care deeply about the bar results. As you begin planning for the bar, be sure to confirm in your mind, and consider committing to paper, all of the reasons why you care enough about passing the bar exam on your first try to give preparation your best effort. Surprising as it may seem, some examinees do not care as much about passing as they could and should. You may hear examinees saying things like they are only *giving it a try* just to *see what it's like*. They may explain that they have a job already, that passing the bar is not critical to retaining the job, and that if they don't pass after only modest preparation, then they will just take it again giving preparation a harder try. Some examinees may say those sorts of things just to cope with the pressure and deal in advance with the potential embarrassment of not passing, when they may be just as devoted to preparing as if their career depended on passing. Let's hope so. Do *not* take the bar exam simply to find out what it is like. The worst thing that you can do to yourself and those who care about and depend on you is to give preparation a half-hearted try. Decide early on that results matter, and treat preparation accordingly.

Visualization

When someone takes on a significant challenge, they should have a sense of what succeeding in that challenge will look like. You chose to take the bar exam. You must have some idea of what passing the bar exam would mean to you and others who care about you. As you begin to prepare for the bar exam, give yourself permission to visualize what passing would look and feel like. Imagine opening the envelope with the letter bearing the good news, or seeing the pass list online with your name on it, or hearing from a friend who is sharing the good news. Consider whom you will ask to sponsor you for admission, which judge will swear you in, and who will attend to celebrate with you. Many times during your preparation, you will need the energy, emotion, commitment, will, and purpose to pull yourself forward toward your goal. Visualizing passing the bar can give you that encouragement. Do not picture the opposite result. Any time that your mind turns toward what *not* passing would feel like, banish the thought, and substitute the positive image for it. Athletes have learned that positive visualization can calm the nerves, slow the heart rate, deepen the breathing, and help you relax and concentrate, which is what you need to do to prepare for the bar exam. If visualization is a challenge for you, then don't hesitate to right positive statements on sticky notes to place around your study space. Right positive notes to yourself or ask a friend or family member to do so.

Waiting

You will not receive your bar results for weeks or months. Examinees often express a sort of puzzlement over that post-bar, pre-results wait. If you are already employed as a law clerk at a court or law firm while you await bar results, then you can more easily distract yourself with that employment than if you are unemployed and looking for work or waiting for results to look for work. During that time, people will ask you repeatedly whether you have the results, when you expect the results, and how you feel that you did. Don't let these questions fluster or flummox you. You are about to become a licensed lawyer. People who have seen you studying for the bar exam, whether family, friends, employers, or prospective employers, expect you to have a new anticipation and confidence after the exam. They want to see you positive and even eager. Some examinees do feel confident about how they did, while other examinees don't feel confidence and may even feel that they probably did not pass. Experience suggests that negative self-assessments are unreliable guides. Of course you will have thought of additional things to add to essay answers and probable omissions and mistakes that you made. Every examinee does think so afterward because every examinee has made some omission or mistake. Don't let recriminations spoil your wait for results. More importantly, don't let recriminations feed the worry of your family members and friends. Find out when to expect results. Then rehearse and use positive answers to the common waiting-for-results questions, even if you feel negatively. Give yourself and others a break.

Transition

Because you will not receive your bar results for weeks or months, you should have a plan for what you will do during that period, beyond that well-earned celebration and break for having completed the bar exam. You may already have employment as a law clerk in the law firm or with the court or agency where you will continue to work after you receive your results and get sworn in. Finding and accepting such a position can be ideal because you will have already embarked on your career and begun your professional development in earnest without the wait. You must not practice law until licensed, but while awaiting licensure, law clerks can do many tasks that are highly useful to clients and law firms. Get started, if you can. If you haven't yet been successful in locating that job, or if you plan and prefer solo practice in any case, then you have *plenty* to do while waiting for bar results. Job search, like planning a law practice, can be a full-time job. Use the weeks or months after the bar exam and before licensure in concerted job-hunt or practice-development mode. In either case, you have *tons* of positive things that you can do. Consider the wait for results an absolute *gift* of time when you can devote yourself fully to your professional contacts and network, and your practice development, full time. Once you begin practice in earnest with your license, you will wish that you had that development time.

Celebration

Then, when you actually get the news that you passed, let yourself be excited. Doing so may take an hour, day, or week. We don't all react in the same way. Yet at some point, be sure to celebrate, and be sure to let those who supported you, particularly family and friends, know that you are celebrating. They need to celebrate, too. Let them see and feel your joy and elation. Feel their joy and elation, too. Laugh aloud, smile broadly, holler if you wish, or weep with joy if you prefer. Just let it go, even if only for a short while.

Swearing In

Simply because you pass the bar exam does not mean that you are now licensed to practice law. State bars typically require that you take the lawyer's oath before a state court judge after receiving your positive results. Your law school or local bar association may plan a swearing-in ceremony within a couple of weeks of the announcement of the results. If so, then notify your school or local bar that you will attend that ceremony so that its administrator can add your name to the list. State bars typically require that a lawyer licensed in the state sponsor your admission at the swearing-in ceremony. Be thoughtful about whom you choose as a sponsor. Invite the lawyer who inspired you, supported you, or acted as a mentor if the lawyer's attending the ceremony would not inconvenience that lawyer. Mentor law professors, at least those whom the state has licensed, are also an option, although consider looking forward toward building contacts and relationships within the profession you are entering rather than looking back to the law school that you are leaving. If you have no one whom you wish to sponsor you, then the ceremony's administrator will have a sponsor available. You may alternatively arrange with the local state court a private swearing-in ceremony just for you and your sponsor. The local courts typically designate a judge to handle those administrative duties. You may also wish to choose a judge who has been your mentor and supporter.

Retake

Among the bar's many examinees, some committed and prepared examinees simply do not pass the bar exam the first time, for a variety of personal or performance reasons. Those examinees may have appeal and re-grading opportunities, which they should promptly investigate. While everyone knows how badly examinees feel for not passing the first time, they should not take not passing as proof that they are unable to do so. Many examinees pass on the second or subsequent try. The biggest key to retake success is to learn from a first effort. Performing the same way that the examinee performed the first time is not likely to be the examinee's key to success. Some examinees don't pass because they ran out of time and did not answer the last question or questions. Those examinees need to better allocate time. Other examinees don't pass because they stated conclusions only rather than applying and analyzing the law. Those examinees need to apply and analyze the law on the next try. Other examinees don't pass because they missed seeing and analyzing big issues. Those examinees need to spend more time issue spotting more effectively. Other examinees lacked any guiding structure in their essay answers. Those examinees need to follow IRAC structure the next time. Examinees should have individual results available to them. They should order and obtain those results immediately, review them closely, and review them with their law professors, commercial bar-prep-course staff, and everyone else they have available with the skill of discerning exam performance.

Conclusion

Perspective

What, really, is the bar exam? Lawyers, law students, law professors, and others actually give several different answers. Most practically, the bar exam is a licensing test. You take the bar exam to get a law license. In that sense, the bar exam is not one last awful punishment inflicted on law students before they hit easy street on their way to a rainbow's end pot of gold. The bar exam is simply something you must do first before you practice law. Keeping the bar exam in that perspective can help. The bar exam is certainly not anything even remotely close to facing combat, indeed not even close to fighting fires or patrolling dangerous streets. Not only is your physical safety never at risk, your preparation and the exam itself are both in relative comfort, with no extreme heat or cold like the millions who work outdoors daily face. You will be well fed at all times and have every other modern convenience throughout. In that sense, preparing for the bar exam and even *taking* the bar exam are both positions of rather extraordinary *privilege*. Treat the whole experience for what it truly is, which is a premier if not *the* premier professional-preparation experience, and you will have gained appropriate perspective.

Growth

The bar exam does more than qualify you for licensure for a highly desirable professional career. The bar exam is also probably the single greatest challenge that a person can choose today to promote one's own development of clear thought and sound reason in pursuit of social, economic, and other good. The bar exam itself may not be the greatest fun, but it can be an indispensable spur to profound development. After the bar exam, you will likely feel differently about yourself than you did when you began bar studies because indeed you *are* different after the exam. You will have studied, organized, digested, and integrated your law knowledge into a highly useful whole. You will have also learned new self-management skills and new skills at reading, summarizing, reviewing, recalling, writing, and analyzing. Your new capacities will serve you well not only in a law career but in life. Yet you will also have increased your appetite for personal and professional growth. Passing the bar exam is not all that you will accomplish. As you recover from the bar exam, you may for a while not think about anything big as your next career or life step. Yet soon enough, you will be looking for that next challenge, and then the one after it, and the next one, and beyond to ever greater pursuits. You will have developed such personal and professional capacities that you will soon yearn to entrust them to appropriate ambitions. After the bar exam, you should relax and celebrate but also know that you will have more to achieve and celebrate in the future.

Outcomes

The one thing that makes the bar exam so frightful for so many examinees is not arduous bar-exam preparation or the conditions of the test itself. You can study intensely for an extended period, and you can manage a two-day test. The experience is nothing even remotely as risky and arduous as military boot camp. No, the one thing that makes the bar exam so frightful for so many is *not passing*. Examinees have several common reasons for fearing not passing, most of them pretty sensible, like the additional wait and cost of taking it again, the examinee's disappointment and embarrassment, the potential loss of a job or job opportunity, delay in hiring, and the disappointment of family and friends. When one thinks about each of these things, though, one realizes that they are each entirely manageable. They are, if you will, *first-world* problems, not third-world problems. *If* they happen, and you have no reason to believe in advance of your earnest preparation that they probably will, you can and will survive them. The other remarkable thing about these concerns, in addition to each of them being not such great concerns in the grand scheme of things, is that with responsible commitment to earnest preparation they are not all that likely. Most examinees who take the bar exam pass the bar exam. Even for those who do not pass on their first try, many examinees who retake the bar exam pass the bar exam on their second or subsequent try.

Alternatives

Law practice is a dream career for many of us. Law students routinely get to taste that dream in the clinical part of their law school curriculum. You have heard how special law practice can be, and you have probably already experienced at least some of that allure. While the sound allure is in law practice's meaning, the benefits of practice are also material. Studies continue to show substantial average increases in earnings with licensure for law practice. Yet lawyers who pass the bar exam often move immediately or soon into other careers, for many different reasons. Law practice under licensure is just one of many careers pursued by those who earn a law degree. Many who earn a law degree never take a bar exam because they have no need for doing so. Your decision to take the bar exam is likely a good to great decision, the outcome of which you largely control. At least, you control many things influencing whether you will pass the bar exam. Other things you cannot control. Life goes on while you prepare for the bar exam, and life may keep you from preparing adequately or even from taking the bar exam at all. Even with your best effort, circumstances may conspire to lead you down a different path than the bar exam and licensure. Keep the perspective that while you value hugely the challenge of taking and passing the bar exam, you are doing more than taking a licensure exam. No matter the outcome, by giving bar preparation and the exam your best, you are proving once again your deepest commitment and faith. Those of us who have prepared for and taken the bar exam have something special to share, something more special than we would have had if we had *not* taken the bar. But for you, as for any examinee, only the future knows just what that special thing is. Keep the bar exam, and preparing for the bar exam, in perspective. For one last help, consider this concluding humorous but true story, contributed by a noble professional who after passing the bar went on to become both a distinguished judge and international mediator. If he passed the bar exam, then you too can pass.

Though he had solid plans for his law career, indeed employment already lined up, the young man had decided to return to his parents' house while studying for the bar exam, where he hoped that he would not only save room-and-board costs but also have the peace, comfort, and familiar social support of a warm and welcoming home. That his beloved younger sister would be at home from college was more consolation than distraction, especially when he was able to make the home's quiet basement his bar-exam command center. And indeed, everything went fine as the bar exam approached until a fire suddenly engulfed the first floor of the home. As the family stood safely outside counting their blessings but shocked at the sudden loss, the young man caught the attention of one of the firefighters. Could he possibly, the young man asked, rescue his precious bar-preparation notes and materials, so critical to his career, from the basement? In through the flames, smoke, and hosed water went the brave firefighter who moments later came back out proudly holding

the sodden and blackened bar materials.
The family took temporary residence crammed
together in a single motel room where the
only study solitude the young man could find
was to hole up in the tiny bathroom.
Uncomfortable sitting on the closed toilet
lid to study, the young man instead slumped
down in the bathtub for hours at a time
poring over his charred, smoke-smelling bar
materials, not the perfect way to prepare for
the bar but yet, as it turned out, wholly
sufficient. He passed, just as you will with
due diligence.

Bibliography

BERMAN, SARA J., PASS THE BAR EXAM: A PRACTICAL GUIDE TO ACHIEVING ACADEMIC & PROFESSIONAL GOALS—TEACHER'S EDITION (American Bar Association 2013);

BUDGET LAW SCHOOL FOR THE BAR, BAR EXAM MENTOR: MENTORING FOR BAR CANDIDATES—TESTED BAR EXAM ISSUES FROM A-Z (2015);

CHARLES RIVER EDITORS, BAR EXAM PREPARATION 101: THE TEXTVOOK (Vook 2011);

DARROW-KLEINHOUSE, SUZANNE, ACING THE BAR EXAM: A CHECKLIST APPROACH TO TAKING THE BAR EXAM (Thomson/West 2008);

DARROW-KLEINHOUSE, SUZANNE, THE BAR EXAM IN A NUTSHELL (West 2d ed. 2003);

EMANUEL, STEVEN L., ED., STEVE EMANUEL'S BOOTCAMP FOR THE MBE: EMANUEL CONFIDENTIAL FOR YOUR LAST FEW HOURS BEFORE THE MBE (Aspen Pubs. 2010);

FRIEDLAND, STEVEN I., THE ESSENTIAL RULES FOR BAR EXAM SUCCESS (Thomson/West 2008);

HOLMES, DR. WANITA, BAR EXAM SUCCESS: USE THE POWER OF YOUR SUBCONSCIOUS MIND TO PASS THE BAR EXAM (2015);

JEFFRIES, RICHARD N., THE CONFIDENCE TO PASS: STUDY TIPS FOR THE UNIFORM BAR EXAM AND ANY BAR EXAM (2013);

KLEIN, JESSICA, THE GOAT'S GUIDE: THE COMPLETE STEP-BY-STEP GUIDE TO PREPARING FOR THE CALIFORNIA BAR EXAM ON YOUR OWN (2013);

MICHAEL, JACK, *A BEHAVIORAL PERSPECTIVE ON COLLEGE TEACHING*, IN THE BEHAVIOR ANALYST 14(2) 229-239 (1991);

NORENIL, CHAD, THE ZEN OF PASSING THE BAR EXAM (Carolina Academic Press 2011);

RACINE, MATT, BAR EXAM MIND: A STRATEGY GUIDE FOR AN ANXIETY-FREE BAR EXAM (2d ed. Lake George Press 2014);

SAIIDI, DUSTIN, THE 7 STEPS TO BAR EXAM SUCCESS: THE STRATEGY GUIDE FOR PASSING YOUR BAR EXAM WITH GREATER CONFIDENCE, IN LESS TIME, AND WITH LESS STRESS THAN THE REST (Saiidi Group 2013);

SPRINGFIELD, DAVID, HOW 2 STUDY LAW: YOUR GUIDE TO BAR EXAM SUCCESS—PROVEN ADVICE, STUDY TIPS AND INSIGHT FOR LAW STUDENTS (Springfield ExamPress 2005);

VALUE BAR PREP, MBE BIBLE FOR THE BAR EXAM (2015);

VALUE BAR PREP BOOKS, PATHS TO SUCCESS FOR CURRENT AND FUTURE BABY BAR EXAM STUDENTS (2015);

WALTON, KIMM, & STEVE EMANUEL, STRATEGIES & TACTICS FOR THE MBE (Wolters Kluwer 2013).

Acknowledgments

The authors are solely responsible for the contents of this book. The authors nonetheless acknowledge Western Michigan University Thomas M. Cooley Law School and its President and Dean Don LeDuc for supporting the mission of legal education to give graduates access to practice including passing the bar exam. The authors also acknowledge Assistant Dean Tracey Brame and Professors Devin Schindler, Chris Hastings, Tonya Krause-Phelan, Chris Trudeau, Mike Molitor, and Tony Flores for reviewing the book's brief treatment of specific law subjects. No law school faculty works harder or more effectively to help its students learn and its graduates pass the bar exam. These outstanding educators, each of them also former premier practitioners, know the law about which they write and speak. The authors also acknowledge and thank Head Librarian Aletha Honsowitz and Reference Librarian Amy Ash for research support and research assistant Jennifer Fields for manuscript review. The authors also thank the Honorable John Fields for sharing the true account from which the authors wrote the concluding story.

About the Authors

Nelson Miller is a professor and associate dean at Western Michigan University Thomas M. Cooley Law School. The Harvard University Press book *What the Best Law Teachers Do* included Dean Miller, who teaches torts, civil procedure, and other courses including bar review, among its 26 featured professors. Dean Miller has presented on legal education and law teaching at national conferences, and published 28 books and dozens of book chapters and articles primarily on law, law practice, and legal education. His books include *A Law Student's Guide, A Law Graduate's Guide, Teaching Law, Dear J.D.: What to Do with Your Law Degree, Lawyer Finances, Entrepreneurial Practice,* and casebooks on torts, civil procedure, and professional ethics. Before joining Cooley, Dean Miller practiced civil litigation for 17 years in a small-firm setting, representing individuals, corporations, agencies, and public and private universities. The State Bar of Michigan recognized Dean Miller with the John W. Cummiskey Award for pro-bono service. He earned his law degree at the University of Michigan before joining the firm that later became Fajen and Miller, PLLC, his practice base before teaching and administering full-time at WMU-Cooley Law School.

Douglas Johnson is an assistant professor of psychology, member of the industrial/organizational behavior management faculty, and Co-Chair of the Industrial/Organizational Behavior Management Graduate Program at Western Michigan University, where he also earned both his Ph.D. and M.A. degrees. His research interests are in organizational behavior management, instructional design, and evidence-based education and training techniques, including computer-based instruction. The founder of Operant-Tech Consulting, Dr. Johnson has consulted internationally with organizations on, and provided services related to, instructional design, training design and development, e-learning, performance management, systems analysis, fluency training, incentives, and feedback and employee motivation from a behavior analytic perspective. He directs Western Michigan University's Instructional Design and Management Research Lab, which uses evidence-based methods to develop and maintain consistent and productive human performance outside of training contexts.

www.ingramcontent.com/pod-product-compliance
Lightning Source LLC
Chambersburg PA
CBHW070728220326
41598CB00024BA/3342